Blond Ambition

The Rise and Rise of Boris Johnson

Nigel Cawthorne

First published by Endeavour Press Ltd in 2015.

Contents

Chapter One – The Birth of the Blond

Before the 2015 election, Boris Johnson wrote *The Churchill Factor*, a biography of Britain's wartime leader, inviting comparisons with the great man himself. Both had trans-Atlantic connections. Churchill's mother was Brooklyn beauty Jennie Jerome. Boris was born in New York, in a low-rent hospital on the Upper East Side of Manhattan. His parents were in the States on his father Stanley's Harkness Fellowship, which funds UK students' studies in America. Stanley Johnson was determined to secure joint citizenship for his son and registered his birth with both the US authorities and the British consulate. So, technically, Boris is eligible to become President of the United States.

His parents had met when they were students at Oxford. Stanley had won the prestigious Newdigate Prize for poetry, once won by Oscar Wilde. Daughter of the bursar of All Soul's, Sir James Fawcett, Charlotte attended the ceremony where Stanley read an extract from his winning entry. They had tea in her halls soon after and married the following spring.

While Stanley had been a staunch Conservative since school, Charlotte came from a long line of liberal lefties, which included leading lights from the Suffragettes and a radical MP who sat in Gladstone's Liberal administration in 1880. Her parents were close friends with campaigners Lord and Lady Longford. Charlotte's mother was a Catholic convert of Jewish extraction. Charlotte herself had been on CND and anti-apartheid rallies, while her brother has worked for the New Left Books before adding a little radical zest to the *Economist*.

Stanley took a course in creative writing – then in its infancy – at the State University of Iowa. Then they returned to New York, where Stanley enrolled on an economics course at Columbia University. They lived in a loft on West 23rd Street, opposite the Chelsea Hotel where Dylan Thomas was staying when he died.

As a condition of the scholarship, Stanley had to travel widely. So in May 1964, when Charlotte was eight months pregnant, they drove down to Texas. Unable to take the car out of the country, they travelled on to Mexico City by Greyhound bus. There they met up with Boris Litwin, a Russian émigré whose daughter Stanley had known at Oxford.

Litwin was appalled that Stanley intended to take the heavily pregnant Charlotte back to New York the way they had come and bought them airline tickets so they could fly back. In gratitude, Charlotte said she would name the baby Boris, whichever sex it turned out to be.

Stanley could not be persuaded to attend more than one of his wife's antenatal clinics and, at the moment of birth, he had popped out for a pizza. The child was born on 19 June 1964 a robust 9lb 1oz and already, at birth, had a disordered mop of platinum blonde hair.

The origin of this is supposed to have been the blond-haired inhabitants of the Turkish village of Kalfat in north-west Anatolia, where Boris's great-great-grandfather had come from. His mother was said to have been a blue-eyed Circassian slave girl.

Boris's great-grandfather, Ali Kemal, was an Anglophile Turkish politician who fell foul of the Nationalists in 1922, during the birth pangs of the Turkish Republic. His first wife who was a half-English, half-Swiss woman had given birth to their son, Osman Ali. She died in childbirth and the boy was brought up by Margaret Johnson in Southbourne-on-Sea, Dorset. Osman Ali became Wilfred Johnson. His son, Stanley, would be another blond.

Boris himself would be christened Alexander Boris de Pfeffel Johnson. In the family, Boris was always known as Al and his first article in *The Times* appears under the by-line Alexander Johnson. The "de Pfeffel" comes from his grandmother, Irène, wife of Wilfred "Johnny" Johnson, who was born in the Versailles home of Baron de Pfeffel. According to BBC's *Who Do You Think You Are?*, Irène was the granddaughter of an actress and Prince Paul von Wüttenberg, a descendant of George II, making Boris an eighth cousin to David Cameron. Granny Butter, as Boris knew her, maintained her aristocratic pretensions to the end and urged Stanley to look into the possibility of claiming a French barony.

Soon after Boris was born, his parents decided to return to England so that Charlotte could complete her English degree. But first, they made a tour of New England and Canada. Throughout it all, Boris was said to have been an unbelievably good baby.

3

Back in Oxford, Boris amused himself while his mother, already seven months pregnant with her second child, prepared for her finals. It was later discovered that he was so quiet and self-contained because he was deaf. The condition, "glue ear", regularly confined him to bed as a child. At the age of eight or nine, the problem was solved when he underwent a series of operations to put grommets in his ears. But his early deafness left him with a curious detachment and a great capacity for reading.

In July 1965, the family moved to Crouch End in north London. After teaching, studying for a Masters in Agricultural Economics and, according to his own account, being recruited as a spy, Stanley was offered a job at the World Bank in Washington DC. But first the family moved to a rented cottage on Exmoor where Stanley wrote his first novel *Gold Drain*.

Moving to Washington in February 1966, they lived for a month in the Dupont Plaza Hotel, before moving into a clapboard house in the northwest of the city. Boris's first memory is of playing in the tree-house in the garden there.

The children were looked after by a series of au pairs, none of whom stayed long, while their parents moved in distinguished circles that included the veteran BBC correspondent Charles Wheeler.

In 1968, as an April Fool's Day joke, Stanley applied for a $100-million loan to finance the building of three more pyramids to boost Egypt's tourist trade. The new president of the World Bank, former Secretary of Defense Robert McNamara, did not see the funny side and Stanley was fired. He got a new job with the Population Council, set up by John D. Rockefeller III in New York. The family lived a house in Connecticut. As part of his work, Stanley travelled a great deal and there were more short-lived au pairs.

There were riots in the US in 1968 and Charlotte wanted to return to England. They flew home the following year and moved to Nethercote in the Exmoor river valley, where Stanley's parents had a farmhouse. His sister also lived there briefly and Stanley's family moved into the family compound. Conditions were primitive.

Stanley loved the place, though he was sent away to boarding school at Sherborne, which he also lauded in his autobiography *Stanley I Presume*. Though poor, his family, he thought, had breeding and a certain class. He claimed never to have met a grammar school boy until he went up to Oxford on scholarship at the age of nineteen. This sense of superiority gave him an arrogance that led him to think it was all right to break the rules as long as you did so in style.

Though Boris resembled his father in many ways, it was said that his intelligence came from his mother. She read to the children and made sure that their interests were literary and highbrow. They were taught to value education and ambition. Boris's own competitive edge was honed when his sister Rachel, just fifteen months younger than him, learnt to read first. As a child he was not content to grow up to be Prime Minister or President, he said he wanted to be "world king".

Cheering him on was Stanley, who flew into a rage if Boris did not outdo his siblings. Coming second would never do, said Stanley, it was emphatically *not* about taking part.

Dinner guests at Nethercote were treated to the spectacle of Stanley and Boris sparring like alpha males, with the younger children finding it hard to get a word in. On one occasion, Boris came to blows with Rachel over the name of the lead singer of The Clash. On another, younger brother Leo shot Boris with an air gun. Though he was rushed to hospital for emergency treatment the incident was treated as a joke in the Johnson household. Nevertheless, the family were close and, after moving frequently as a child and now cut off in a remote farmhouse, Boris found it difficult to make friends outside the family.

In 1969, Stanley got a grant from the Ford Foundation to do post-graduate research at the London School of Economics and the family moved to a house in Maida Vale, rented from a friend of Charlotte's parents. Taking time off from study, he joined the Conservative Research Department where he met up-and-coming Tory grandees Douglas Hurd and Chris Patten.

When Stanley headed off around the world researching another book, the family went back to Nethercote, where Boris went to Winsford Village School. After Stanley returned, they bought a home in Primrose Hill, London NW1, and Boris attended Primrose Hill Primary School, later the alma mater of both David and Ed Miliband. Thanks to a windfall – Stanley complained that he had always been dogged by good luck – the family moved into a larger house nearby to accommodate the brood that had now swelled to four.

Their next move was to Brussels, where Stanley exercised his environmental concerns as head of the Prevention of Pollution and Nuisance Division of the European Commission. At the European School in the outlying suburb of Uccle, Boris met a girl named Marina Wheeler, daughter of Charles Wheeler and his Sikh wife Dip. She had just arrived from Washington and impressed Boris with her "Impeach Nixon" badge. On the other hand, she decided he was "generally to be avoided" and the Johnsons were "wild and out of control".

At the European school, Boris was identified as a gifted child. But at home things were going badly wrong. Charlotte was having a nervous breakdown. Suffering from depression, she spent nine months in the Maudsley Hospital in London, where Boris and the other children would visit her. After that, she was in and out of hospital quite often and, even when she was at home, she did not seem entirely well.

Boris and Rachel took over the role of child care of their younger siblings. Rachel was cast as Wendy to Boris's Peter Pan, with their two younger brothers, Jo and Leo, playing the Lost Boys.

Chapter Two – Boarders

In September 1975, eleven-year-old Boris and Rachel, then ten, were packed off to Ashdown House, a prep school in Sussex. The children would make the trip there themselves. Before the era of Eurostar, they would be dropped at the Gare du Nord in Brussels with a packed lunch and take the train to Ostend. They would take the ferry to Dover, then the train to Victoria. After a stop at the Cartoon Cinema – though Boris later favoured the British Museum – they would take the train to East Grinstead. The journey would take the whole day.

Once, returning at the end of term, they managed to get on the train bound for Moscow instead of the one for Brussels. Again, the event was treated as a comedy rather than a potential catastrophe.

Just before Christmas in 1978, Charlotte and Stanley separated. Stanley took the blame. It was his constant philandering that had caused the split. The au pairs were a particular target. Boris recalled how, in the hot summer of 1976, they used to walk around temptingly naked. He later confided that, after his parents had split, he decided to make himself emotionally invulnerable.

Boris's parents divorced when he was fourteen. The family home was sold and Charlotte moved into a flat in Notting Hill, where she became a portrait painter. Sitters included Joanna Lumley and Jilly

Cooper. Though she was short of money, the children often used to stay with her and she found Boris very supportive.

In 1988, she married an American academic and moved to New York, returning a widow in 1996, again living in Notting Hill. By then she was suffering from Parkinson's disease.

Boris found school life at Ashdown House "idyllic", except for one thing – the regular beatings he received from masters. He became a vehement opponent of corporal punishment. It was the one of the few subjects he was said to talk seriously on.

"I remember being so enraged at being whacked for talking at the wrong moment that it has probably given me a lifelong distrust of authority," he wrote in 2009.

At Ashdown House, Boris – already a P.G. Wodehouse fan – began creating his persona of a bumbling English eccentric of 1930s' vintage, though some of it must have been borrowed from his father. He also excelled academically, particularly at Latin and Greek, and won a King's Scholarship to Eton. At sports, he was not so gifted, but he was an enthusiastic rugby player. This lent him a certain physical assurance.

In 1979, Stanley was elected Conservative MEP for Wight and Hampshire East. Soon after, he met Jennifer Kidd, a left-leaning former editor at Weidenfeld & Nicholson. They married in 1981 and she gave him two further children, Julia and Maximilian, both of whom were blonds. This brought with it a new round of sibling rivalry.

Chapter Three – Eton Mess

Having entered Eton as a King's Scholar – even though he had scraped in thirteenth – Boris was one of the intellectual elite and his hair made him instantly recognizable. However, he was not among the social elite, known as the Oppidans, who had got there by dint of money.

After a term mucking in with the Oppidans, Boris was given a room in College, the Scholars' house. Dating from the Middle Ages, it was the oldest building in the school. The regime there was more liberal than the true-blue houses where the fee-paying boys lived. The denizens were known as "Tugs", because of the gowns –"togas" – Scholars must wear at all times. Nevertheless, Boris was quickly inculcated into the school's ethos that Etonians were groomed to be future leaders, duty-bound to repay society for the privileges that had been bestowed on them. Clearly, Old Etonians were destined to rule over others.

Among the Scholars, Boris did not distinguish himself, but he was certainly much brighter than the other boys. His house master David Guilford, who also taught him Classics, called him "an all-rounder, very good at rugby and the Wall Game, but perhaps less at cricket. He was a School figure – unusual for a Scholar."

Guilford also taught David Cameron but remembered nothing of him, though Cameron was considered "posh" by contemporaries, even by the standards of Eton.

Determined to stand out, A.B. – Al or Alex – Johnson slowly became the more distinctive "Boris". Desperate to fit in, he abandoned his mother's Catholicism for the Church of England and, while his new-found poshness was a mere façade, he pulled it off with humour and perfect comic timing.

Boris was perfectly in tune with the times. Michael McCrum had become headmaster in 1970. He favoured academic excellence over social cachet. Fagging and caning were being phased out.

While spotty and swotty, Boris shone during debates, even deflecting difficult questions from masters. His performance in Maths and Science was not good, but he excelled in Classics.

After a shaky start in English, he went on to win the English prize, developing his familiar style in the school magazine, *The Chronicle*. When the former Prime Minister visited the school's Political Society, which Boris later ran, he wrote: "Edward Heath was lit up from behind, his face in the shade and a halo of silver light extending from his temples, like a prophet of old."

Boris's style is notable again in a spirited defence of privilege he wrote in December 1980: "I tell you this. The Civilized World can ignore, must ignore these idiots who tell us that by their very existence public schools demolish all hopes most cherished for the Comprehensive System. Clearly, this is twaddle, utter bunkum, balderdash, tommyrot, piffle and fiddlesicks of the most insidious kind. So strain every nerve, parents of Britain, to send your son to this educational establishment (forget this socialist gibberish about the destruction of the State System). Exercise your freedom of choice because in this way you imbue your son with the most important thing, a sense of his own importance."

Three years later, in an interview with *The Chronicle*, Ken Livingstone, then leader of the soon-to-be-abolished Greater London Council and later Boris's rival for Mayor of London, gave a riposte.

"I think your school," he said, "should be integrated into the state system, because I don't think you have the right [through] what your parents can buy [to] a privileged start over the rest of society. I look at the people who have emerged from Eton and Harrow, Oxford and Cambridge and I think you're a load of bloody wallies."

The young Boris's awards included the Newcastle Classical Prize, though his masters complained about the lateness and presentation of his work. It was said that he lacked a "commitment to the real business of scholarship". A report sent to his father mentioned his "disgracefully cavalier attitude", his "sheer feckless" and "gross failure of responsibility" despite being "surprised at the same time that he was not appointed Captain of the School".

"I think he honestly believes that it is churlish of us not to regard him as exceptional," it went on, "one who should be free of the network obligation which binds us to everyone else."

The author also mentions that he is "enormously fond of Boris" and praises his performance in the College play where he played the comic figure Sir Politique Would-be. There was even talk of him going to Harvard.

Later, the same teacher complained: "Boris is pretty impressive when success can be achieved by pure intelligence unaccompanied by hard work. He is, in fact, pretty idle about it all. Boris has something of an tendency to assume that success and honour will drop into his lap…"

He was even forty-five minutes late for a meeting with the provost. When the provost, naturally, took offence, Boris said it was because he wanted to invite Ronald Reagan to speak at the Political Society.

The report continued: "It was perhaps a bit of a risk to make Boris Captain of the School: but he clearly has the personality and the respect necessary for the job…"

The master later explained that, despite appearances, Boris was not a rebel at all. "He was a fully signed up member of the tribe. He was jolly nearly the custodian of the ark. Everything that went into the traditions of being at College, Boris embraced whole-heartedly – Latin prayers, bellowed hymns."

Boris also came to the fore in the Wall Game, which pitted the Scholars against the Oppidans. While protesting against the Vietnam war conducted by US President Lyndon Baines Johnson, he chanted: "Hey, hey, LBJ, how many kids did you kill today?". *The Chronicle* ran: "Hey, hey, ABJ, how many Oppidans did you kill today?"

It also told spectators to "watch the blond Behemoth crud relentlessly through the steaming pile of purple-and-orange

14

[Oppidan] heavyweights". His own wild disregard of his safety and that of others when playing rugby was also noted.

Recklessly ambitious, he also became editor of *The Chronicle*, bringing in a coterie that included Andrew Gilmour, son of Sir Ian Gilmour, then Privy Seal in Margaret Thatcher's government; Darius Guppy, later jailed in an insurance swindle; and Viscount Althorp, later Earl Spencer, brother of Princess Diana. At parties at Althorp, Boris rubbed shoulders with genuine toffs, giving a decided leg-up to the first-generation Etonian – Sherborne was not considered top-draw. Boris went on to become a member of "Pop", Eton's self-electing elite. They wore checked, spongebag trousers and waistcoats, and were above the admonitions of masters.

But Boris did not just cultivate aristocrats. He made friends with the few black pupils there were at Eton, who were otherwise ignored. Then there were girls.

As secretary of the Debating Society, he organized trips to girls' schools for competitions. He was already star of the debating team, and some were picking him out as a future PM. One female contestant was particularly impressed as Boris seemed to knock up his speech after arriving at the venue, scribbling it on a piece of paper on the back of a tree.

Boris spoke in favour of the motion "This House would Emigrate" in 1981, when Mrs Thatcher's economic policies had decimated British industry and laid much of the country to waste. On that occasion, he lost the vote.

Boris was rarely a loser, though music was not his forte. Determined to triumph in the piano competition, he set about trying to learn the instrument. Though he struggled manfully, he did not have the co-ordination, failing Grade 1 despite "months of brow-beating effort". Years earlier, he had been bested on the recorder by his sister Rachel. And later, he was ousted from a rock band when he failed to master the opening bars of "Smoke on the Water" on the bass guitar.

A new headmaster took over at Eton in 1980. This was Sir Eric Anderson, who had previously been Tony Blair's housemaster at Fettes. He spotted a similarity between the two boys.

"Both of them opted to live on their wits rather than preparation," he said. "They both enjoyed performing. In both cases people found them life-enhancing and fun to have around, but also maddening."

Famously, when Boris was playing the lead in *Richard III*, he could not be bothered to learn his lines, so he pasted them on the back of various pillars. He spent the performance dashing from pillar to pillar, fluffing his lines and causing much amusement – except to the rest of the cast who had learnt theirs.

Anderson once gave Boris's sixth-form class ten minutes to write down what the words "business, industry and commerce" suggested. Boris's essay was succinct.

"These words suggest to me that the headmaster dined in London last night," he said. He was right. Anderson later said that Boris was the most interesting pupil he had ever had.

"Anyone who's spent an hour with Boris never forgets it," he said.

Whatever his shortcomings, Boris could not have been faulted in Classics and won a scholarship to Balliol College, Oxford – normally considered the home of "lefties", and not the natural habitat of High Tories such as Trinity, Christ Church or Magdalen, where his mates Althorp and Guppy went.

On his page on Eton's College Leaving Book, Boris put a picture of himself toting a machine gun and note of his ambition to put "more notches on my phallocratic phallus". In fact, he saw Oxford as the place he would find the pick of potential wives. Once married, he thought, he could get on with the serious business of his career.

Chapter Four – Bullingdon and Beyond

Boris spent his gap year teaching English and Latin at Geelong Grammar School – Australia's Eton – at the Timbertop campus where Prince Charles had spent two terms. A sojourn digging latrines for starving children in Africa was not for Boris.

It is unclear whether Boris dabbled in drugs around this time. On occasions, he has admitted to puffing on the odd joint. Once, on *Have I Got News for You*, he said he had even been offered cocaine – "but I sneezed and so it did not go up my nose. In fact, I may have been doing icing sugar". Since Bill Clinton's admission that he had once smoked a joint but "did not inhale", it has been important for politicians not to seem completely out of touch, while not alienating Middle England – or, indeed, Middle America.

When Boris arrived at Balliol in the autumn of 1983, Oxford was still basking in the reflected glory of the TV series of *Brideshead Revisited*, which had its own blond hero, Lord Sebastian Flyte, played by Anthony Andrews. It was packed with other OEs who ran their own "invitation only" clubs. One such was the Bullingdon.

Putatively founded in 1780 as an all-male sporting club, its membership was limited to thirty. Boris, David Cameron and George Osborne were all members, though Boris, with his comparatively modest background, was way down the pecking order.

Over the years, it had become a dining and drinking club and its drunken antics were legendary. Once, when a pot plant was thrown through a restaurant window, Boris claimed to have joined the others overnight in a police cell. No charges were pressed. Some doubt whether he was actually there. But it seems that he signed up to this Bertie-Woosterish prank anyway – though at the *Telegraph* Max Hastings compared him to newt-fancier Gussie Fink-Nottle.

Others note that Boris does not like to be out of control, either on drink or drugs. Nor, like his fellow members, could he afford to pick up the tab for the damage done. It was the Bullingdon way to trash the place, then buy their way out of the consequence. Boris did not have that sort of cash behind him.

What he did need, though, was for the other Old Etonians to stand behind him. Though the university had made some efforts to be more egalitarian during the 1960s, it was still home to toffs. They looked down on anyone who was not from the three top-line public schools – Eton, Harrow and Winchester – again as "Tugs". Those from grammar schools were "Stains". Beyond that, alumni of comprehensive schools were simply beyond the pale.

Boris expected other OEs to gather round when he made his first bid for power. However, he turned up half-an-hour too late to put his name down for a position on the Treasurer's Committee of the Oxford Union. This did not stop him running for the prestigious position of secretary the following summer. The OEs won it for him. This gave him a platform to run for president of the Union, which, in earlier times, was seen as a sure stepping stone to the top in politics.

Standing against him was a grammar-school boy Neil Sherlock – a Stain. But Boris had a secret weapon. He had bagged a prestigious girlfriend, Allegra Mostyn-Owen. She was the daughter of Christie's chairman Willie Mostyn-Owen, OE – a descendent of Owen Glendower, the last Welsh prince of Wales – and his socialite wife Gaia. They had a stately home, Woodhouse, in Shropshire and a seventeenth-century castle Perthshire – Gaia once admitted she had no idea of how many rooms it had.

Not only was Allegra fiercely intelligent – studying Politics, Philosophy and Economics at Trinity – she was a sought-after beauty. Terence Donovan photographed her for *Vogue* and David Bailey got her on the cover of *Tatler*. Boris won her with his typical style. Hearing that she was having a party, he turned up a night early with a bottle of wine, saying he had mistaken the date. She did not know him, but she had been reading a dusty book on economics and invited him in. They drank the bottle of wine and chatted. He made her laugh. They became friends. Then he indicated that, unless they became an item, he would have to spend more time on his work at the Union. He was soon the envy of every heterosexual man at the university and this prize raised his social standing considerably.

Allegra also had other uses. When Boris was running for the presidency, she invited Neil Sherlock to tea in her rooms and implored him not to impede the progress of her beau. Despite her obvious charms, Sherlock's head was not turned and he smelled a rat when Boris turned up as he was leaving. Plainly, Boris was desperate and traditionally you are not supposed to canvass for votes

21

in Union elections. But while Boris could depend on the support of the OEs, he overstepped the mark handing out free bottles of wine to prominent members of the constituency. This was simply not done. He appeared to be trying too hard and Sherlock won easily.

Boris was shocked. This setback shook his OE sense of entitlement. Even at Oxford, it seemed, a toff could no longer trump trade. For this brief interlude at least, it seemed the class war had been lost.

During the summer vacation of 1985, Boris and Allegra went on a tour of Portugal and Spain with Rachel and her boyfriend Sebastian Shakespeare. To fund their contribution to the trip, Boris and Rachel decided to produce a report on animal cruelty for the World Wildlife Fund, secured through Stanley. They researched bullfighting, the mistreatment of donkeys and the use of monkeys as props by beach photographers.

Allegra's contribution was her contacts. Wherever they went, instead of staying in some grotty B&B, she found a local aristo or oligarch to put them up.

Though Boris was only twenty-one, it was clear he had made his mind up to marry his princess. But he did not pass muster with her family. Her father found him "rapacious" and "wilfully scruffy", while Gaia scared him. When he went skiing with the family, Boris left his passport behind so had to catch a later flight. When he turned up, he found the only thing in his suitcase was his dirty sheets from Balliol. He had to ski in his normal clothes – moleskin trousers and a tweed jacket – like an Edwardian gentleman. He also told Allegra's mother that he could not ski, then impressed her with his daredevil antics.

Allegra and Boris had one thing in common. They were both fiercely competitive.

"They used to compete on everything, even down to who had the best orgasm," a friend said.

It was clear to one and all that Boris and Allegra were, albeit unofficially, engaged. For ever-ambitious Stanley, Allegra was something of a catch. However, he managed to dampen the ardour of Sebastian Shakespeare, and Rachel went on to marry a genuine blue-blood named Ivo Dawnay.

Back at Oxford, Allegra became editor of the student magazine *Isis* with Rachel and Darius Guppy in tow, while Boris threw himself back into student politics. He now realized that, to get elected, he had to broaden his appeal beyond his core OE voters. Steering clear of Guppy, he was now everyone's friend. He learned another lesson. When it came to the business of garnering votes, he must not appear too gritty or thrusting, or too party political. But it was easy for Boris to hide his overweening ambition under a cloak of Johnsonian buffoonery.

Briefly the Social Democratic Party, or SDP, had made an appearance in national politics. Boris let everyone think he was a supporter. He also employed "stooges" – one of whom was Michael Gove – and he co-opted American student Frank Luntz, later a successful pollster in the US, to analyse the electorate. Disregarding Luntz's advice to stick with Reagan-Thatcher conservatism, Boris was determined to be everything to everyone. He was into conciliation rather than Thatcherite confrontation. He even spoke up for proportional representation. Boris won with a thumping majority and the national newspapers began running pieces about the new president of the Oxford Union and his eye-catching girlfriend.

It is generally agreed that Boris did not do much with the Union once he had won the presidency – other than use it as a stepping stone for a future career in journalism. He invited Max Hastings, editor of the *Daily Telegraph*, and Anthony Howard, a family friend and deputy editor of the *Observer*, to speak, while he held sway as from the speaker's chair.

Allegra encouraged this because, to preside at debates, Boris had to turn out in evening dress, rather than his usual shabby attire. However, Union staff kept a bottle of Tippex on hand to paint over the stains that regularly appeared on his shirt-front.

The role of president attracted a certain amount of female attention. Women offered to wash his clothes for him and buy him shampoo – things that Boris was, evidently, too busy to do. To hold on to her man, the aristocratic Allegra had to take on these menial roles.

As president of the Union, Boris got his first taste of power. The Union had a staff of fourteen and a turnover of a quarter of a million pounds. Boris held sway over this empire from the thirty-foot long, book-lined office – which he would hardly match as Mayor of London.

As soon as the term of office was over, Boris abandoned his SDP credentials. The stooges who had helped him were ruthlessly abandoned. At the 1987 general election, he proudly donned the blue rosette again. Some of his contemporaries accused him of having no political beliefs at all. Boris agreed. Apart from "vague sensations of enthusiasm when the Falklands were recaptured," he said, "I did not give a monkey's … I had viewed politics with a perfectly proper mixture of cynicism and apathy. Whatever I read under the bedclothes, it certainly wasn't Hansard."

Then, he recalled being asked to contribute towards the miners, who were on strike. For Boris, it was an epiphany: "… as I reached for my pocket, I found myself remembering some stuff I'd read about these miners, and the chaos they were causing with their illegal strike," he wrote twenty years later. "Oi, I said to my fellow-student. No, I said. I won't give any dosh to these blasted strikers, because, as far as I can see, they are being execrably led, haven't had a proper ballot and are plainly trying to bring down the elected government of the country."

When Stanley Johnson went up to Oxford in the 1960s, he had set himself three goals – to win a Blue at rugby, to become president of the Union and to get a first. He achieved none of these. Likewise, Boris had set himself three goals – to find a wife, to become president of the Union and get a first. He had succeeded in the first two. Now he settled down to work on the third. In earlier terms, Boris had winged it. At tutorials, where students were expected to read out their essays, Boris would appear empty handed and ad lib.

Once his presidency was over, though, he disappeared into the library and set about swotting, but missed a first by a hair's breadth and had to settle for the top 2:1 in his year.

Chapter Five – Boris Goes to Brussels

Boris and Allegra married at St Michael and All Angels, West Felton on 5 September 1987. While she looked stunning, Boris failed to find anything suitable to wear and had to be lent a pair of trousers by Tory MP John Biffen. Unfortunately, his shoes did not fit and Boris had to keep on his own battered footwear.

At the reception at Woodhouse, the composer Hans Werner Henze – a gay German Marxist – gave the world premiere of his piece "Allegra e Boris". His previous compositions had lauded Che Guevara and Ho Chi Minh. Anna Steiger, daughter of Claire Bloom and Rod Steiger, sang an aria from *The Marriage of Figaro*. The confetti were sugared almonds.

Rings were exchanged but, by lunchtime, Boris had mysteriously lost his. He had also lost the wedding certificate which was found, months later, in the pocket of Biffen's trousers. Reflecting on his own youthful marriage, Stanley remarked they were "lambs to the slaughter".

Allegra is thought to have paid for their honeymoon in Egypt. They then bought a flat in a converted Victorian house in Olympia, west London. Boris took a well-paid job with a high-flying management consultancy and bought a pair of red braces, standard kit in the post-Big Bang City of London. He was not well suited to the job.

"Try as I might, I could not look at an overhead projection of a growth profit matrix, and stay conscious," he said.

Boris stayed just long enough to collect his joining fee and, after a week, left. But he was so well connected that, with the highest recommendations, he walked straight into *The Times* as a graduate trainee. They sent him on a three-month secondment to the *Express & Star* in Wolverhampton to learn the business of reporting.

Allegra's own journalistic career, spent largely on the *Evening Standard*'s Londoner's Diary column, was soon to have a setback. She and Boris had written a piece for the *Sunday Telegraph* about Olivia Channon, daughter of Trade and Industry Secretary Paul Channon, who had choked on her own vomit in the Oxford rooms of Gottfried von Bismarck. It included details of a lunch where Tina Brown, who in 1984 had moved from editing the *Tatler* in London to *Vanity Fair* in New York, tried to extract the "tasteless details" of Olivia's death. The piece appeared under Allegra's by-line, but it was Boris who had been at the lunch. That allowed Tina Brown to dismiss the whole article as fiction. Allegra quit journalism.

Boris returned to London without a good report from the West Midlands. *The Times* moved him onto the desk rewriting copy from the news agencies. On his one opportunity to visit the frontline – a National Union of Seamen's strike in Dover – Boris fled back to the newspaper's Wapping headquarters at the first opportunity.

More trouble ensued when an archaeological dig in London unearthed the lost palace of Edward II, where Boris said that the King had cavorted with his catamite Piers Gaveston, quoting, ostensibly, his godfather Dr Colin Lucas of Balliol. However, Gaveston was executed in 1312 and the palace was not built until 1325. Lucas, who was aiming for a professorship in Chicago as a stepping stone to the vice-chancellorship of Oxford, had not been interviewed and protested that he would not have made such an elementary mistake.

Boris wriggled on the hook, but it was plain that he had made up the quote – a sacking offence on *The Times* in the 1980s. Boris still blames "fact-grubbing historians" for his downfall. Nevertheless, through Max Hastings, he walked straight into a job as a leader writer on the *Daily Telegraph*. It was Boris's spiritual home.

He was no newsman though. Boris had attended the wedding of Earl Spencer, along with the Prince and Princess of Wales. The Peterborough column heard that best man Darius Guppy had failed to deliver the traditional speech. When Boris was asked to confirm this, he "blustered [and] did the wobbly blancmange act".

However, when called upon, he would sweep aside the coffee cups, sandwich wrappings and papers that cluttered his desk and, occasionally strutting up and down, produced seamless copy to a deadline, so clear he was in his opinions.

"I've only seen a few people – Max Hastings, A.N. Wilson and Robert Fox – write like that under pressure," said features writer Bernice Davison. "It's an amazing feat of concentration, being able to produce 1,200 or 1,500 flowing words without a trace of the angst it would cause most of us."

Meanwhile junior staff and undergraduates on work experience were dragooned to bring coffee, tea, sandwiches and research material. And Boris spent his time honing his unique style. He does not pepper his column with Woosteresque anachronisms such as "crumbs" and "cripes", though there is that perception of him which he does little to challenge. However, he addresses his readers as "my friends", as if co-opting them. His enemies are also addressed as "my friend", to disparaging effect.

True, he plays the fogey, but his pieces are cleverly crafted. He takes a specific event from his slightly elevated lifestyle, or an object, such as a worn out ski glove, then weaves a story out of it, usually one that charms those of a right wing persuasion. The story is used to illustrate a point that is, for a dyed-in-the-wool Conservative, slightly left-wing in its sentiment. He is marvellously inclusive. Here is the fool making a sensible, well-argued point, and a standard-bearer for the right, making a point that would not sit badly with a bleeding-heart leftie. For example, while the rest of the Conservative Party run scared of Nigel Farage on immigration, Boris shrugs and says that, while some people are naturally afraid of it, we need to get used to it. It is the consequence and wellspring of Britain's success.

However, Boris's pieces were frequently spiked because they were late. He also liked to play the fool around the office. So in 1989, he was sent to the *Telegraph's* bureau in Brussels. He knew the city, having spent some of his childhood there, and could speak good French and Italian, along with some German and Spanish. The salary was good, but Boris insisted on extra money for uprooting his wife. When she had finished her law exams that summer, Allegra followed him to Brussels – after all, he needed someone to do his washing and cleaning. Otherwise, she saw little of him.

To start with, the posting seemed a poisoned chalice. News emanating from the Brussels bureaucracy was by and large dull. But then Mrs Thatcher took up cudgels against the EU and the Berlin Wall fell, along with the Soviet Union. The re-unification of Germany was about to redraw the map of Europe and Boris was the man on the spot.

As a reporter, Boris was hopelessly out of his depth, but other members of the press corps were happy to lend a hand. His father still lived and worked in Brussels and could engineer key introductions. Geoff Meade, from the Press Association wire service, recalled being invited to Sunday lunch by Stanley. During aperitifs, a taxi crunched to a halt in the driveway and out jumped the stunning Allegra and Boris in the world's loudest pair of Bermuda shorts. In a city known for its sober elegance, Boris was known for his eccentric attire.

Seeing him in one particularly shabby suit, one French journalist enquired: *"Qui est ce monstre?"*

When nothing else worked, Boris fell back on clowning. At press conferences, he would ask questions in comically bad French, even though he could speak the language well. He was always on show. Even when he darted around Brussels in his bright red Alfa Romeo

31

with its doors held on with string, he had AC/DC blaring on the stereo. He demanded attention.

Boris soon spotted that the EU press corps was rather too cosy with the bureaucrats they were reporting on and went out of his way to shake things up. He took up the Eurosceptic cause, which had formerly belonged to Tony Benn and those on the left. Boris made Eurosceptism the property of the right, largely by making fun of the EU's decisions and institutions.

"Changes in the rules governing crisps and sausages could so easily symbolize the threat posed by Brussels to the British way of life,'' he wrote.

"EC cheese row takes the biscuit," ran one headline.

Egged on by Max Hasting, who urged him to "be more pompous", he was the acknowledged master of the "straight banana" school of EU reporting, and his stories became essential reading for Mrs Thatcher as well as other journalists. Other newspapers carried stories about him. He even had influence, though it was acknowledged that his stories were not always accurate.

Well known for not being the most assiduous checker of facts, Boris was fed a wholly untrue rumour to see if it surfaced in a Johnson story. It did.

He even announced that the commission headquarters in Brussels was to be blown up after asbestos had been found. Blowing it up would only have spread the danger. Instead, the building was extensively refitted and still stands.

His favourite target was Jacques Delors, president of the European Commission from 1985 to 1995. After the signing of the Maastricht treaty, but before it was ratified by the member states, the *Sunday Telegraph* ran a speculative piece by Boris on the front page under the headline "Delors Plan to Rule Europe".

"Cor, I thought," Boris wrote later. "That was a bold way of expressing it, and I wasn't sure that my chums in the EC commission would be thrilled. But the splash was the splash – the main article on the front page – and I happily consented. That story went down big. It may not have caused the dropping of marmalade over the breakfast tables of England, but it was huge in Denmark. With less than a month until their referendum, and with mounting paranoia about the erosion of Danish independence, the story was seized on by the 'No' campaign. They photocopied it a thousandfold. They marched the streets of Copenhagen with my story fixed to their banners. And on June 2, a spectacularly sunny day, they joyously rejected the treaty and derailed the project. Jacques Delors was not the only victim of the disaster; the aftershocks were felt across Europe, and above all in Britain."

The no vote was a body-blow to Delors. At a press conference afterwards, it was said "the pallor of his skin suggested he had received an electric shock".

Delors tried to fight back, but Boris's wit gave him the upper hand.

"We answer his attacks," said one frustrated EU official, "but the problem is that our answers are not funny."

Politicians feared the press conferences he attended and tried to "Boris-proof" their policies. It is even thought that Foreign Secretary Douglas Hurd put pressure on Max Hastings to have him sacked. Hurd has denied this, but claimed to have chummed up with fellow Eton King's Scholar "to keep him off my back". Boris reciprocated with vitriolic attacks. The Foreign Office was said to have dedicated a team to rebutting his stories, or having them spiked in the first place.

While the government struggled to maintain its position in Europe, Boris always managed to put it on the back foot. After a long day's negotiation, Hurd always dreaded the press conference afterwards with Boris there in the front row, preparing to throw a grenade.

Then came the most seismic political event in Boris's world – the ignominious ousting of Margaret Thatcher.

"After it was all over, my wife Marina, claimed she came upon me stumbling down a street in Brussels, tears in my eyes, and claiming that it was as if someone had shot Nanny," he wrote later. "I dispute this…"

As well he might, as he never had a nanny and he was still married to Allegra at the time. But people who knew him always took his stories with a pinch of salt. He was not a person of conviction like Thatcher, nor was he nearly as Eurosceptic as he made himself out to be – particularly because his father worked for the Commission. Far from being anti-European, Boris was suspected of being a closet federalist.

It was an act. He would work himself up for bilious rants by locking himself in his office and hurling a torrent of abuse at his yucca plant. Once he had achieved peak frenzy, he would rattle out his piece at machine-gun speed, beating the keys with his fist. If anyone interrupted, he would yell furious expletives at them.

Back in Britain, these rants were stoking the Euro debate that was tearing the Conservative Party under John Major apart. Boris later explained on *Desert Island Discs*: "I was sort of chucking these rocks over the garden wall and I listened to this amazing crash from the greenhouse next over in England as everything I wrote from Brussels was having this amazing, explosive effect on the Tory Party. And it really gave me this, I suppose, rather weird sense of power."

This would eventually make the party that he supported unelectable for over a decade.

John Major accused Boris of being obsessed with Europe. It was true. His war with Delors consumed him, leaving little time for a home life. Often he would jump on a plane in pursuit of a story. Allegra would have to phone the foreign desk of the *Telegraph* to find out where he was.

"You get past caring and you start drinking malt whisky," she said. And she feared she was going to have a nervous breakdown.

The straw that broke the camel's back was when Boris came home one night and asked her what she thought about "subsidiarity" – the latest entry to Euro-lexicon. She packed her bags and flew back to London.

Boris was distraught. In the aftermath, he was seen drunk. It was very rare for him to even have more than a few glasses of wine, though often he would use a mythical "hangover" as an excuse for lateness or ill-preparedness – then he could fire off with his mind as sharp as ever.

Normally not a clubbable person, Boris turned to his colleagues for support. This was a surprise for them. He was usually very secretive, never known to open up. While other journalists hunted in packs, Boris was a lone wolf and his aloofness was often taken for arrogance.

Chapter Six – Boris Unbound

While the divorce was in progress, there was a reconciliation. Allegra had begun studying for her Law Society finals, but flew over to Brussels at the weekends. Then she enrolled at the Université Libra de Bruxelles for a Masters in EU law. This had been recommended to her by Boris's old school-chum Marina Wheeler, who had taken the course the previous year.

Not only had he been enamoured of her when they were at the European School together, they had dated briefly when they were sixteen. He had discovered that you could get a free lunch at the Hare Krishna centre in Soho.

"I thought the food was delicious, but she didn't think much of it and has never forgiven me," said Boris.

She was a public school girl too, but had gone to the laid-back co-educational Bedales whose alumni included Sophie Dahl, Gyles Brandreth and Daniel Day-Lewis. Then she studied Law at Fitzwilliam College, Cambridge

Marina was living nearby in Brussels and Allegra would invite her around for dinner. But when Allegra was away, Boris began pursuing her. He was not a man who could manage on his own and he always craved female company. Though Marina was a left-winger and Boris's high Tory views were an anathema to her, she found herself falling in love with him.

Soon after Allegra left for good, Marina fell pregnant. By then she and Boris were engaged. They seemed a better match. While Allegra had sought to change Boris, Marina accepted him the way he was.

Despite Boris's general ineptitude with paperwork, the divorce was rushed through. Marina and Boris married in Horsham town hall and had a low-key reception in the garden of the Wheelers' house nearby. It could hardly have been more different from his first wedding. Marina kept her maiden name and the honeymoon was one night in a hotel in East Grinstead. He had been a bachelor for just twelve days.

Back in Brussels, they moved into a house. But otherwise things had not changed. When Marina went into labour she had to call the *Telegraph*'s foreign desk in London to track him down. Boris was at the coast, covering the story of a ship that looked like it might sink and he insisted on filing it before flying to the side of his wife. He celebrated the birth with a piece headed "Congratulations! It's a Belgian."

As both Boris and Marina had been born abroad, their daughter did not automatically inherit their nationality. In the article he begged the Home Secretary Michael Howard not to let her become a Belgian by default, saying: "Do you wish to see her claimed by a nation which refused to sell us ammunition in the Gulf war? Shall she scamper, her face gleaming with chips and mayonnaise, as thousands of Bruxellois did the other day, to watch the National Day firework display, her heart beating at the sight of the black-red-yellow flags?" She was registered as a British subject five years later.

Marina wanted to call their daughter Lara; Boris preferred Lettice. As a result, she was christened Lara Lettice, but is known as Lara. Fatherhood did not dent Boris's 24/7 work schedule and he was as driven as ever, writing for the *Telegraph*, the *Sunday Telegraph* and their sister publication, the *Spectator*.

In one piece, he rued the state of the modern British male – "his reluctance or inability to take control of his woman and be head of a household". *Private Eye* carried a repost, saying: "These moral lectures sound a little odd when one learns that Johnson had to arrange a quickie divorce from his first wife, Allegra Mostyn-Owen, after discovering that he had impregnated his lover, Marina Wheeler. Johnson's belief that a man should take charge in the household scarcely tallies which his own domestic habits. He is notoriously reluctant to pay for anything (he wasn't even prepared to foot the bill for his first honeymoon) and is almost incapable of dealing with income tax, insurance policies and other such duties that often fall to the head of the household. 'The modern British male,' Johnson concluded in the *Spectator* last week, 'is useless.' Speak for yourself, matey."

The source for this story was, allegedly, Allegra herself.

Others confirmed his meanness. He did not buy drinks or take people to lunch, and acquaintances were warned never to lend him money as he did not pay it back. He was also eager to borrow – or lift – other people's stories, give them his own spin and outshine the original with his splash, but got away with it with flattery and charm.

After four years in Brussels, Boris's charm was wearing a little thin on both EU officials and other journalists. As he packed his bags, James Landale of *The Times* wrote a valedictory modelled on Hilaire Belloc's "Matilda", about a girl who tells lies:

Boris told such dreadful lies

It made one gasp and stretch one's eyes.

His desk, which from its earliest youth

Had kept a strict regard for truth,

Attempted to believe each scoop

Until the landed in the soup.

In the parody, Boris says that Britain is going to pull out of the EU, and the other correspondents have to follow his lead as there is no time to check the facts, then are forced to retract when Douglas Hurd and John Major deny it. Then the other journalists become sceptical.

For every time he said "Delors' the Messiah",

We only answered: "Nah, it's a flyer."

In journalist speak, a flyer is a speculative piece based on guesswork rather than facts. The lampoon concludes:

The moral is, it is indeed.

It might be wrong but it's a damn fine read.

Boris sent a note, thanking Landale for the poem.

Back in London, Boris began looking for a new stage on which to parade his talents. He fancied becoming a war correspondent, but the *Telegraph* decided that his habit of being economical with the truth might prove dangerous in a combat zone. Besides, Boris was a notoriously big spender on his expense account and sending him somewhere where he could not be reined in might bankrupt the paper.

Even the column he got reviewing cars on *GQ* was said to be the most expensive in magazine history. He would casually double-park the latest high-powered "babe magnet" outside the Royal Festival Hall or New Scotland Yard. As a result, parking fines would build up "like drifting snow on the windshield". More than once, a junior had to be sent around to fetch it back from the car pound.

Back in London, Boris wanted to live in Notting Hill where Rachel lived. It was soon to be home to David Cameron and other up-and-coming Tories. But, at Marina's insistence, they bought a house in Islington, home to Tony Blair and New Labour.

Illustrating the political gulf between them, when asked how he formulated his right-wing ideas, Boris said he asked what Marina and her family thought on any subject then turned 180 degrees – "I can't go wrong."

Although they were living in what Boris would consider enemy territory, that area of Islington was a "media gulch", full of TV producers and journalists, though usually of a liberal bent. And while the area is affluent and gentrified, it was close to the bad lands of Holloway, so crime was an ever-present worry.

Marina had given their new house a contemporary look with stripped-pine floors, while Boris contributed the old-fashioned mess. When an American journalist came to do an interview for *Vanity Fair*, he found Boris in his underwear, bumbling around looking for his trousers. Suspecting that the scene may have been contrived, Boris, he wrote, "quite clearly invites underestimation".

The Johnsons needed a large house. Their first son, Milo Arthur, was born in 1995, Cassia Peaches in 1997 and Theodore Apollo in 1999 – these last two had their father's colouring, while Milo and Lara were honey blondes. None of them inherited any of their mother's dark, half-Indian looks.

The children went to Canonbury Primary. When Boris played celebrity auctioneer at the school fundraiser, other local celebs contributed lots that included Chris Martin of Coldplay playing in your living room and a guided tour of the House of Lords by Lord Adonis. The event raised tens of thousands.

Not that Boris was uncritical.

"I have children in state primary education, and I have to tell you that times have changed," he wrote. "They call the teachers by their first names, which was not the case when I was in state primary education. The teachers have no power whatsoever to discipline them, terrified as they are of the great engine of state retribution if they are felt in any way to have infringed the rights of the child."

When it came to secondary schooling, Boris was not embarrassed to go private, though he admitted that the middle-class flight from state education compounded the problems of the schools they left behind.

Naturally, Boris wanted to send his sons to Eton. But Marina put her foot down. She did not want another Old Etonian in the house and her doggedness had a profound influence on his thinking. For example, when Lord Macpherson of Cluny's report into the death of Stephen Lawrence found "institutional racism" in the Metropolitan Police, Boris dismissed this, at first, as "Orwellian" – in, of all places, the *Guardian*.

A year later, he wrote in the *Spectator*: "I have had savage arguments with my nearest and dearest, and, slowly, I have begun to see things his way ... The Laird of Cluny is no loony."

Boris so frequently lost to the liberal-left arguments of Marina in the domestic debating chamber that he began calling her "M'learned wife", while she called him her "fifth child".

In the *Evening Standard*, Boris claimed to be a "careerist nappy-changing MP-cum-journalist-cum-househusband", but it is clear that most domestic chores are left up to Marina, who also has a high-powered career as a lawyer to maintain. Not for him "ridiculous compulsorily paid paternity leave".

Admittedly, with their joint salaries, the Johnson's could afford to hire a house keeper, cleaner, a nanny and a couple of au pairs.

Boris's musings on whether women really want to work so hard, and blaming women graduates for everything from the rise in house prices to mugging, drew the charge of sexism.

"Obviously a Neanderthal corner of my heart worries about some aspects of the coming feminization," he admitted. "Will we all become even more namby-pamby, elf-n-safety-conscious, regulation-prone and generally incapable of beating the Australians at anything than we already are?"

The children did not see much of their workaholic father, but when they did it was fun. A *Sun* reader snapped him test driving a 195mph Lamborghini Gallardo Spyder for *GQ* magazine with his two sons in the front seat of the sports car. He took his rugby-mad son Milo to Twickenham, played tennis with the boys on a Sunday morning and, when a family holiday to Greece was nearly scuppered when they turned up late at Luton airport, Boris jumped on a windowsill in the departure lounge and made a cash offer for tickets, eventually parting with £2,000 for two extra seats they needed on the EasyJet to Athens.

Boris was criticized by fellow parents for being "eccentrically liberal" by letting his children watch the James Bond movie *For Your Eyes Only*. He compounded the charge by admitting that they also watched *Hot Fuzz* and *Shaun of the Dead*. But then one of Boris's frequent targets are Puritans.

The Johnsons' attitude to parenting was outlined in a book of verse called *Perils of the Pushy Parent – A Cautionary Tale*, written and illustrated by Boris. It continues such gems as:

Loving parents, learn from me.
If your children crave TV
Tell them, OK, what the hell
You can watch it for a spell…
IF YOU READ A BOOK AS WELL.

The *Guardian* called it "the most cringe-making book every published". Boris's next-door neighbour in Islington was Ian Katz, then a senior editor at the *Guardian*. Boris would make regular protests about his treatment by that left-leaning newspaper by leaving his copy on Katz's doorstep.

But Boris was not that liberal a parent. He came out against Nintendo, Game Boy and PlayStation, citing "the catastrophic effect these blasted gizmos are having on the literacy and the prospects of young males".

"They sit for so long that their souls seem to have been sucked down the cathode ray tube," he said. "Steel yourself for the screams and yank out that plug," he urged. "And if they still kick up a fuss, then get out the sledgehammer and strike a blow for literacy."

Chapter Seven – Blond Ambition

Boris's despatches from Brussels had damaged the Conservative government. He enjoyed all the attention this brought him in what he admitted was a "babyish way". There was factional fighting between the pro- and anti-Europe wings of the Conservatives and the whole party was mired in "Tory sleaze".

Boris had had his own brush with scandal. Darius Guppy and a business partner had themselves tied up in a New York hotel room, making it look like they had been robbed of £1.8-million jewels in an insurance fraud. When Stuart Collier from the *News of the World* looked into the case, Guppy called Boris asking for Collier's address so he could have him beaten up. Boris did not give him the address, but the call was on tape and he seemed sympathetic to his friend's plan. When Guppy was jailed for the insurance scam, Boris still praised him in the *Telegraph* for living "by his own Homeric code of honour, loyalty and revenge". Soon after a tape of the telephone conversation was sent to Max Hastings, Boris was summoned and chastised. Only later did a transcript appear in the *Mail on Sunday*. By this time, Boris was a forthright champion of law and order. He told the *Mail* that it was "all a bit of a joke".

At the age of just thirty, Boris was made an assistant editor on the *Telegraph* and chief political columnist.

"I'm a bit worried," said Boris about the appointment. "I don't have any political opinions."

When pushed, all he could come up with was: "Well, I'm against Europe and against capital punishment."

The new editor, Charles Moore, said that Boris performed the task with "maximum idleness". Paul Goodman, former *Telegraph* comment editor, recalled an editorial meeting where Boris was asked what he was going to write that day.

"Aaaarrrrgggghhh! Cripes! Erm …" said Boris.

"Well?"

"I thought … sort of … eeerrrhhhmmm."

"Sorry?"

"I mean … um … Blair."

"What about him?"

"Sort of … gosh! … Europe … and …"

"And?"

"Hague … I mean, Hague! … er … sort of …"

"So, I'm to tell the editor that you're writing about sort of Blair, Europe and Hague, sort of?"

"No … well … un … Yah! … er … That's it!"

Nevertheless, a few hours later, an "immaculately composed and piratically arresting essay would appear".

On another occasion, he asked Northern Ireland Unionist leader David Trimble a typically waffling question at a crucial Belfast peace conference and Trimble replied: "Fuck off Boris."

But he found always found something both amusing and trenchant to fill his column. Now up to speed on everything European, he found a worthy adversary in Tony Blair's spin doctor Alastair Campbell and, in 1997, won "Commentator of the Year" at the "What the Papers Say" awards.

However, having Boris annoying people out in Brussels was one thing, having him bumbling around the *Telegraph*'s building in London was quite another. He began to get on people's nerves. Even his use of language was guaranteed to grate. He talked of "coolies" and "piccaninnies". The problem with Africa was "not that we were once in charge, but that we are not in charge anymore," he said. Even in the face of the credit crunch, he defended the rich.

"We seem to have forgotten that societies need rich people, even sickeningly rich people, and not just to provide jobs for those who clean swimming pools and resurface tennis courts," he wrote. "Without them there would be no Chatsworth or Longleat."

Like a posh version of Jeremy Clarkson, he set out to offend virtually everyone, but got away with it through wit and charm.

"Islam will only be truly acculturated to our way of life when you could expect a Bradford audience to roll in the aisles at *Monty Python's Life of Mohammed*," he said.

"They say [Tony Blair] is shortly off to the Congo. No doubt the AK47s will fall silent, and the pangas will stop their hacking of human flesh, and the tribal warriors will all break out in watermelon smiles to see the big white chief touch down in his big white British taxpayer-funded bird."

"Do you really mean to say the [British] empire wasn't a good thing? … The best fate for Africa would be if the old colonial powers, or their citizens, scrambled once again in her direction; on the understanding that this time they will not be asked to feel guilty."

Palestine? "If we were Israelis … we would dispatch an American-built ground-assault helicopter and blow the place to bits. Then we would send in bulldozers to scrape over the remains, and we would do the same to all the other houses in the area … this is the best way to deter Palestinian families from nurturing these vipers in their bosoms, and also the best way of explaining to the death-hungry narcissists that they may get the 72 black-eyed virgins of scripture, but their family gets the bulldozer."

Then there was: "Whenever George Dubya Bush appears on television, with his buzzard squint and his Ronald Reagan side-nod, I find a cheer rising irresistibly in my throat." However, he later reined back, saying: "It's just maddening that when asked to form a simple declarative sentence on child literacy the leader of the free world is less articulate than my seven-year-old."

And at a Gay Pride dinner, he said: "I'm delighted that as of this autumn any young man will be able to take his chum up the Arcelor Orbit and marry him." Elsewhere, for football fans, it was "up the Arsenal".

"The chicks in the GQ expenses department – and if you can't call them chicks, then what the hell, I ask you, is the point of writing for *GQ*." In the *Spectator*, he claimed to have invented the Tottometer – "the Geiger-counter that detects good-looking women".

Like Clarkson, Boris built a constituency on television. Both have appeared on *Have I Got News For You?* On his first appearance as a panellist in 1998 the Darius Guppy tape was sprung on him. In the *Spectator*, he complained of being "stitched up" and called the show a fraud, claiming that, while appearing to be ad-lib, the lines were meticulously prepared.

Nevertheless, he quickly made up with fellow panellist Ian Hislop, editor of *Private Eye*, who said of his complaining column: "What a load of bollocks, Boris – you must have knocked that out in twenty minutes."

"No, it was shorter than that," Boris replied.

"I expect you were pissed as well," said Hislop.

"I might have been," said Boris. One of his familiar tactics was to disarm the critic by admitting the charge, even when he was not guilty.

The next time he appeared on the show he made an endearing apology. Then he faced a barrage of questions about Iain Duncan Smith, then Conservative Party leader. Boris could not answer a single one of them, which made him all the more endearing.

In the wings, he once asked Hislop: "Do you know what the Tory policy is on immigration?"

Hislop said he didn't.

"Neither do I," said Boris.

When he was asked to be a guest presenter, he pulled it off in typical bumbling fashion. According to Hislop, most presenters spent two days rehearsing. Boris "turned up at six p.m. on the day and had never read the script, which he proceeded to read in that dazed way of his. His insouciance was extremely funny."

Again he used self-deprecation to win the audience over.

"My speaking style was criticized by no less an authority than Arnold Schwarzenegger. It was a low moment, my friends, to have my rhetorical skills denounced by a monosyllabic Austrian cyborg."

On one occasion, his mobile phone rang. He answered it, saying: "I can't talk now, I'm on the television."

Some suspect that this, too, was contrived. Making no apology for his seeming incompetence, Boris said that the real shocker was "not that people are so foolish as to appear on TV, but that people are so idle as to watch it."

Besides, he got £1,000 a time, which was enough to take his kids skiing. And he realized that to succeed he had to appear on shows that people actually wanted to watch; otherwise, "you just stick on Andrew Neil's late-night yawn-a-thon, then you're never going to get anywhere".

His other credits include *Parkinson*, *Question Time*, *Breakfast with Frost* and *Top Gear*. He even had his own two-part TV series, *Boris Johnson and the Dream of Rome*, where he tried to discover how the ancient Romans managed to run a united empire and why the European Union has failed to pull off the same feat. Even when he was being erudite about ancient history – could any other politician do that? – Boris kept the trademark haystack hair which is deliberately messed up immediately before the cameras roll.

The television brought him to a wider audience. He also got star treatment at the paper. Charles Moore would ring him half-an-hour before deadline to find he had not even started his column – or even decided what it was going to be about. He often delivered late, but somehow persuaded the editor to put it in. It was, perhaps, lucky Boris wrote so seamlessly that his copy needed little editing. Nor did he like his prose being tampered with. He typically delivered fifty words short of the required length, so that no one could take a word out.

Boris, of course, made light of his tardiness.

"Dark Forces dragged me away from the keyboard, swirling forces of irresistible force and power," he quipped.

Boris was also inept at his other duty, commissioning comment pieces when Simon Heffer was away. To complete his own column, other journalists found their brains comprehensively picked.

On the few occasions he was put in charge of the paper when Charles Moore was not there, Boris wandered around looking completely baffled. He had not bothered to find out what the job entailed and assumed that, like a well-oiled machine, the paper would run itself. Essentially, he depended on others to do the job for him. Once he even gave a memory stick along with an email address to a complete stranger at an airport and got him to file his copy for him.

There is one thing you can depend on Boris for, Charles Moore once said, and that is to let you down. That was partly because the affable Boris will always say yes to things he had no intention of doing. And he always got away with it with a handful of jokes and ladles full of charm.

Despite his joking around, Boris longed to be taken seriously and had long harboured political ambitions. Since 1993, he had been looking for a seat, initially in the European Parliament, but John Major threatened to veto his candidacy. Then in 1997 he stood as Tory candidate in the unwinnable seat of Clwyd South, dutifully learning the Welsh national anthem and how to order fish and chips in Welsh. He read up on farming and the Common Agricultural Policy, and even won some admirers in the local constituency. Nevertheless, his efforts were doomed.

"I fought Clwyd South, as we candidates put it – and Clwyd South fought back," he said later.

That was the year the Conservative Party suffered its worst defeat since 1906. However, the big beasts of the Tory party who had been rattled by Boris's Eurosceptic attacks from Brussels began to leave the stage, and in 2000 he was selected for Michael Heseltine's rock solid Conservative seat of Henley. For this he had to thank Andrew Mitchell, who eventually fell from power in "Plebgate".

There was one slight problem with his selection. In 1999, Boris had been appointed editor of the *Spectator* on the condition that he would give up looking for a seat in parliament. When proprietor Conrad Black discovered a couple of months later that Boris had sought selection in two different constituencies, he hauled him in and asked him to explain himself.

Boris resorted to his old tactic of simply coming out with his hands up. He admitted that his conduct was outrageous and that Black was within his rights to sack him. He went on to convince Black that he could edit the magazine and be an MP at the same time. Black succumbed to his charm.

As Boris himself said: "My policy on cake is pro having it and pro eating it."

Others were worried that Boris was up to the job of being editor in the first place – even without the added responsibility of representing a constituency. Journalist Andrew Grimson said making Boris editor of the *Spectator* was like "entrusting a Ming vase to an ape". Boris made him the magazine's foreign editor, an unpaid position that allowed him to file copy from as far away as Hackney and Surbiton – and, on one occasion, Burnley.

Prime Minister Tony Blair had called Boris to Number Ten to congratulate him personally on this appointment. Perhaps he thought Boris would continue the demolition job on the Conservative Party he had begun in Brussels.

BBC Radio Four's *The Week in Westminster* almost immediately dropped him as a presenter. Boris claimed that it was because he had a posh voice and "lacked the chameleon skills of Tony Blair who knows how to perform the perfect glottal stop and drop an aitch on *Richard and Judy*."

Black's chief executive Dan Colson was also angry that Boris had persistently lied to him, saying that he was not seeking a parliamentary seat. After Colson had vented his spleen, Boris convinced him that he could edit the magazine part-time. After all, with all his other media commitments, that was what he was doing anyway. Indeed, one of his first acts as editor had been to take two weeks paternity leave. He continued writing columns for the *Telegraph*, *GQ*, appearing on radio and TV, and writing the novel *Seventy Two Virgins*, which was published in 2005.

However, with Boris's hand on the tiller, sales of the *Spectator* were already climbing and it was making money. So Colson sent in minders, including old Fleet Street hand Stuart Reid who made sure the magazine came out on time. And when things went wrong, Boris was not around to shoulder the blame.

"Quite easy, this magazine editing lark," Boris was overheard saying.

Life at the *Spectator*'s Doughty Street offices was like a war room during a major crisis, with Boris missing interviews, speeches and deadlines and often with people dragooning to cover for him at the last moment. Sometimes, at the eleventh hour, when there was no alternative, he would dash off a piece himself.

"Because I have no time to do it, I do it in no time – you just whack it out," he told the *New York Times*.

The show was kept on the road by Boris's Yorkshire-born secretary Ann Sindall, who played "pantomime Northerner" to his "pantomime toff". She dealt with unpaid bills, parking tickets, complaints, tax demands, members of the Johnson household and fended off people trying to find out where he was – even sewing up a rip in his trousers on one occasion. She did all this, it was said, "with the implacable demeanour of a headmistress trained by the SAS".

Amidst this chaos, Boris said he had "more fun than is strictly proper". He rarely came in before lunchtime. There were long, liquid lunches, pretty young women and ping pong in the garden. Editorial meetings were largely an opportunity to swap jokes. The door to the editor's office was always open for anyone who wanted to read the paper or just have a lie down. Above it all was a bust of the Athenian statesman Pericles.

Although the *Spectator* is the voice of Conservatism, Boris allowed all shades of opinion to flourish, even employing the left-wing cartoonist Steve Bell from the *Guardian* whose work he much admired. Irate leftie Rod Liddle also had his say. Against this, Boris kept on Greek-born journalist Taki Theodoracopulos, whose casual racism in his "High Life" column even drew complaints from Conrad Black.

Boris himself ran a leader under the headline "Long Live Elitism", saying: "Without elites and elitism, man would still be in the caves." But in turn he stuck up for asylum seekers and economic migrants. He also hired Andrew Gilligan, who left the BBC after he had claimed that the British Government had "sexed up" a report on weapons of mass destruction to exaggerate the capabilities of Saddam Hussein in the run-up to the Iraq war.

Veteran theatre critic Sheridan Morley was fired in favour of Oxford chum Toby Young who said he knew nothing about the theatre. Earl Spencer penned a diary. Nicky Haslam, Anna Ford and

Joan Collins all contributed, along with numerous members of the Johnson clan, including sister Rachel, brothers Leo and Jo, father Stanley, father-in-law Charles Wheeler and brother-in-law Ivo Dawnay, along with Paul Johnson and Frank Johnson who are not related.

Though getting a good salary himself, Boris was notoriously parsimonious when it came to paying his contributors. Five hundred pounds was top whack, but pieces were to be short. They were to take no more than forty-five minutes and three calls.

When an undercover reporter from the *News of the World* ensnared the Earl of Hardwicke into supplying cocaine, which got him suspended from the Conservative Party, Boris struck back by getting his chum Lloyd Evans to sell the tabloid the inside story of the drug den at the *Spectator*, with Boris himself as both a dealer and a heavy user. The *NoW* smelt a rat.

Evans was then taken on as poetry editor with a salary of one case of cheap plonk every six months. To make ends meet, Evans sold a story to the *Mail on Sunday* about a group of greens having lunch at the *Spectator*. House rules were that the guest list was secret, encouraging diners to speak freely. One of the guests, Zac Goldsmith, complained. Boris phoned Evans to upbraid him.

"Here's the bad news," he said. "You're fired as poetry editor."

There was a pause.

"Now the good news – you're reinstated."

Evans was even promoted.

Boris, the arch rule-breaker, liked journalism to incite. When David Gardner of the *Financial Times* filed a piece on Hindu fundamentalism, Boris told him to "give it more oomph".

"I want to see newsagents go up in flames," he said.

Boris himself outed Dominic Lawson, previous editor of the *Spectator*, as an agent of SIS. When he phoned to complain, Boris said: "I just did it for a laugh."

There were other problems with the sister publication, the *Telegraph*, who were supposed to have the first option on any *Spectator* article. Instead, Boris would sell any likely piece to the *Daily Mail*. When Colson called Boris to complain, Boris eventually phoned back to say: "I cannot believe I've been so monumentally stupid. I should be immediately sacked, my pay confiscated retrospectively, marched out to the square outside Canary Wharf, hung, draw and quartered on the flagstaff." Colson could not get a word in.

Conrad Black got the same treatment. When he called to complain about an article, Boris said: "I am on the top of the most dangerous piste in Gstaad, staring into the face of death, about to decide, depending on why you are calling me, if my intention is to survive my next run or not."

Sometimes things got out of hand. When Petronella Wyatt launched an attack on the Marian Fathers' Polish boarding school at Fawley Court, it drew protests from the Polish ambassador, Catholics and local bigwigs. But Fawley Court was on the borders of his Henley constituency and the election was just nine months away, so he sent out scores of grovelling letters and went to apologize in person.

With the election less than a month away, Boris set his sights on a larger target – Edward Heath, the Tory Prime Minister that had taken Britain into the EEC before getting bumped by Margaret Thatcher.

"It would be utterly magnificent if I could tell you, my friends, that Sir Edward, at 84, has got over his Incredible Sulk and become a piping geyser of optimism about the party under whose banner I am about to fight. Alas, amigos, it is not to be," wrote Boris. "From the moment we sit down at the table, with his belly cantilevered between us like some decked whale, it is clear that he is in no mood to boost my morale … Here we are, two fat Balliol blonds, and the older one wants to rock the confidence of the younger. Well, I won't let him."

Chapter Eight – Bo Selecta

Boris was not a shoo-in at Henley. The Europhile Heseltine certainly did not want to give up his seat to the standard-bearer of Euroscepticism. However, because of his notoriety on *Have I Got News For You?*, the president of the local branch of the Conservative Party invited him to stand. Boris's application came in a week late. Nevertheless, it was accepted.

The front-runner was lawyer David Platt, who was considered to be on the Conservative Party fast-track. Then there was leading woman lawyer Jill Andrew. Both were word perfect in party policies and had been tramping the constituency. On the night of the final selection, Boris was nowhere to be found. However, the car park of the hall where the vote was being held was packed with the upmarket cars of those who had come to see him because he was a celebrity. The vote was a forgone conclusion.

Boris was his usual shambling figure but, because he had been to Eton and Oxford, that was all right. When asked a question about the NHS, Boris said that when Marina had been sleeping after giving birth he had eaten his wife's toast. He was disgusted that the nurses were unable to bring her more toast when she woke up. That's why the NHS needed reforming.

And that was it, his only thoughts on a serious issue. But he had delivered the knock-out punch. He had mentioned that he had a wife and children. Rumours were circulating that David Platt, who later married, was gay and that, at university, Jill Andrew had drunk too much and had been a little promiscuous – cardinal sins in the eyes of the members of the Henley Conservative Association. She was even accused of being a friend of Cherie Blair.

After claiming he had no skeletons in the cupboard, Boris was asked about Guppygate.

"This chap felt he had me skewered, and for one terrible millisecond it seemed he might be right," Boris said. "What he forgot was the volatility of the audience and their sense of fair play. His question was so long, and so venomous, and so full of recondite detail about a decade-old non-scandal, that by the end of it I guess some people were rather hoping I'd be able to bat the ball back."

Which he did.

He had been accused of keeping the Guppy business a secret. But he had been questioned about it on a TV show with an audience of millions – "I don't think you could get much more public than that."

The questioner was booed. Later he received abusive letters and was hounded out of the association.

Even so, the selection went to a second vote. But, as the evening dragged on, the ladies of Henley who turned out for Boris stayed on until, finally, the blond bombshell was selected.

Now editing the London *Evening Standard*, Max Hastings changed his Wodehousian analogy, writing a leader warning Boris that: "To maintain his funny man reputation, he will no doubt find himself refining his Bertie Wooster interpretation to the point where the impersonation becomes the man."

But first he would impersonate Heseltine, who had famously brandished the parliamentary mace at left-wingers singing the *Red Flag* in the House of Commons in 1976. Boris did it rather more modestly with Henley Town Council's version at the Mayor's Annual Dinner, guaranteeing him front-page coverage in the *Henley Standard*.

When the election was called in mid–May, Boris ducked out of all his journalistic commitments and went on the stump. His campaign was criticized for being chaotic. But thanks to *Have I Got News For You?*, he was recognized on the doorsteps.

The *Sunday Times'* A.A. Gill, who accompanied him on the campaign trail, said that he eyed a baby as if it were "Sunday lunch". Over sausage and mash, he has a choice of mustard, "English or French – sound or soft on Europe. The knife hovers. Oh dear, he's gone for the French. 'You must come and write for *The Spectator*.' And then he thinks. 'Oh crikey, that's your story, isn't it? How I tried to bribe you with a column on *The Specci*. Damn, damn.'"

Gill concludes: "Boris Johnson is without doubt the very worst putative politician I've ever seen in action. He is utterly, chronically useless – and I can't think of a higher compliment."

Nationwide, the Conservatives did nothing to dent the Labour majority, but Boris won in Henley, albeit with a reduced majority.

"Go back home and prepare for breakfast," he told his supporters.

Covering the count, Anna Ford asked: "How can you expect to look after this constituency when you can't even look after yourself?"

However, the bookies were already giving odds on Boris becoming the next leader of the Conservative Party.

Conrad Black and his wife Barbara Amiel hosted a victory party for him in their Kensington mansion, replete with cardboard cut-outs of Boris. The French ambassador, another guest, compared the event to the cult of Pol Pot.

Boris went on to sell the serialization rights of his book on the campaign, *Friends, Voters, Countrymen: Jottings from the Stump*, to *The Times* – the newspaper that had once sacked him – before offering it to the *Telegraph* that had come to his rescue. Charles Moore was put out as he paid his wages. It was also noted that, when Conrad Black turned up at *Spectator* parties, he passed unnoticed. Boris was the star of the show.

In parliament, things were different though. Another of the new intake was David Cameron, who immediately went onto the prestigious Home Affairs committee, a showcase for new talent. Boris was relegated to the standing committee on Proceeds of Crime Bill, which had 462 clauses to grind through. He was often late – hearings started at nine sharp – or did not turn up at all.

With the Conservative defeat in the election, leader William Hague stepped down. Boris was expected to back Michael Portillo, though Mrs Thatcher had gone cold on him. Boris had once lauded Iain Duncan Smith as the "future of Conservatism". Instead, inexplicably, he backed Europhile Ken Clarke, even throwing the weight of the *Spectator* behind him.

Clarke's opinion was so diametrically opposed to Boris's that this caused some to enquire whether Boris believed in anything. He answered his critics in his 2003 book *Lend Me Your Ears*, saying: "Here, in these articles, is how I think we should be: free-market, tolerant, broadly liberal (though not, perhaps, ultra-libertarian), inclined to see the merit of traditions, anti-regulation, pro-immigrant, pro-standing on your own two feet, pro-alcohol, pro-hunting, pro-motorist and ready to defend to the death the right of Glenn Hoddle to believe in reincarnation."

Although in the House of Commons Boris was now a little fish in a big pond, he was still the editor of the *Spectator*, had his column in the *Telegraph* and appeared regularly on TV – and his motoring column in *GQ* meant that he regularly turned up in the members' car park in a Ferrari or a Bentley. While other members might be jealous, some of his constituents in Henley considered him, because of his other commitments, a part-time MP. Before the election, after all, he had said he would step down from the editorship of the *Spectator* and quit the *Telegraph*. Now he told the *Henley Standard* that he had taken a pay-cut at the *Spectator* because of his reduced role there – though he was still on full salary. His promise to Conrad Black to quit the *Spectator* if he got elected was also broken.

He defended his position by pointing out that both Winston Churchill and Benjamin Disraeli had supported themselves through writing. Like them, he said, he felt destined to lead his country.

Just when the strain was proving too much for him, he discovered the joys of jogging, taking a half-hour run each morning – making a delightful picture for any photo-journalist who might be door-stepping him. He also began to cycle, again showing his genius at re-branding his image. Despite all this exercise, at 5 feet 10, Boris can still swell to 17 stone – not a healthy BMI.

Jogging and cycling further strained his already creaking agenda, but as Boris explained: "The fatal thing is boredom, so I try to have as much on my plate as possible."

This meant he did not have the time, like other new members, to seek advancement working the tearooms and bars of the Palace of Westminster. But he was not very good at schmoozing. That was David Cameron's forte.

What Boris did manage to pull off was to get a large office to himself, rather than share like other members. His staff were housed on the floor below. They were overworked. His secretary Melissa Crawshay-Williams had to cope with a mailbag twice as big as that of other MPs.

In his maiden speech, Boris followed in the parliamentary tradition of praising his predecessor.

"As many in south Oxfordshire and elsewhere have not hesitated to point out, Michael Heseltine is a hard act to follow," he said, "so I approach this moment with much the same sense of self-doubt as Simba in *The Lion King*. For the benefit of those who have not seen Walt Disney's film, there is a poignant moment when Simba, following his father Mufasa across the veld, compares his own paws with the vast paw prints left by that great beast. Such are my feelings today…"

It has been pointed out that, in the film, Mufasa is killed and Simba flees, pursued by hyenas, only to return to take his rightful place as Lion King and restore the lands to their former glory.

"…I have no arboretum in south Oxfordshire, merely a sort of lopsided laurel. I struggle to run one magazine, whereas Michael told me that at the last count he had 267."

Heseltine was the owner of Haymarket Publishing and his arboretum featured in a BBC Two documentary in 2005.

Johnson said that as Environment Secretary, Hezza liberated many from the captivity of council housing; when Defence Secretary, he stood out against unilateralism under Soviet threat, and in the 1980s helped regenerate Liverpool and the East End of London.

His constituency, Henley, Boris went on, was "like a land of dreams". He said when one stood at the cutting just below the M40's junction 6 – "the Khyber Pass of the Chilterns" – one had the same vision of beauty seen by Thomas Hardy's *Jude The Obscure*. Then there were "the Wittenham Clumps which were famously painted by Constable, and the towers of Didcot power station which were not". Watlington had a first-rate fish-and-chip shop, while the historic village of Ewelme "has the claim to be the centre of English literature and language, as Chaucer's niece is buried there".

There was also had a serious side to his speech. He pointed out the damage foot and mouth had done to the area, and the many rural pubs and post offices that were closing.

"There are pockets of genuine deprivation, problems of poverty and problems of posterity," he said. "For every affluent estate agent in south Oxfordshire – there are quite a few – there are dozens, if not hundreds, of young people who cannot afford housing in the area and whose needs must be attended."

The decline of rural pubs and communities was spurred on by "the punitive measures taken by the police" over drink-driving. So Chancellor Gordon Brown "should offer a tax break to Brakspeare's 2.5 … One can drink three pints of it without coming near exceeding the limit."

Johnson did not often speak in the House – only twice in his first five months. He appeared for around half of the votes and was ranked 525th out of the 659 MPs for attendance. But then, within four months of entering the chamber, on top of his other journalistic commitments, he published *Friends, Voters, Countrymen*. His attendance slipped further in his second term and he rebelled against the Tory whip five times.

Boris was not at home in the House of Commons. He was mercilessly teased for being an Old Etonian, mussing up his hair behind the speaker's chair and having to rush off to put the next edition of the *Spectator* to bed. What's more, the gritty northern Labour MPs on the opposite benches were not his natural audience. Classical references did not impress them; nor did his bumbling Bertie Wooster routine.

"People think I have a bumbling eccentric veneer which hides the fact I am a genius," he said. "I think it is the other way around."

Boris openly admitted his performance in the Commons was "crap".

"I'm not yet world statesman class, frankly," he said. "I've soldiered away on committees, yes, and asked oodles of questions. But they [the sketch writers] don't report them."

Meanwhile, he was at war with the party leadership. He even commissioned Steve Bell to produce a cover showing Michael Portillo pissing on party leader Iain Duncan Smith's head. But IDS needed Boris, who was so popular around the country that he could, by then, command a £25,000 appearance fee. Fan clubs were set up by Home Counties mothers and students at Durham University. He had a greater reach than any other politician. Telling *GQ* magazine why its readers should vote Tory, he said: "Your car will go faster, your girlfriend will have a bigger bra size. It's an attested fact that, under Conservative governments the quality of living of the British people has immeasurably improved, leading to better denticians, higher calcium consumption, leading inexorably to superior mammary development."

Such statements were a ploy he admitted, cloaking a serious intent.

"If you clown around, you may be able to creep up on people with your ideas, and spring them on them unexpectedly," he said.

Unable to discipline Boris, IDS tried to co-opt him. He was to attend the party leader on Wednesday mornings to help him prepare for Prime Minister's Questions. But this failed to curb the wayward Boris. In 2002, the *Spectator* made Tony Blair their Parliamentarian of the Year. He was, Boris said, "the coolest cat in town" – when

Labour benches threaten to rebel, "he quells them as Zeus quelling a bunch of sea-nymphs".

However, his admiration was not unalloyed. He added: "This was a politician who opposed the Falklands war but who has now sent British forces overseas twice on successful engagements."

When chastised for this award by Tory grandees, Boris blamed others on the staff who had given Blair "not the wooden spoon, not the booby prize, but the Top Gong". Nevertheless, Boris was still called in to coach IDS for PMQs, alongside David Cameron and George Osborne who were more committed. Wednesday was press day at the *Spectator* and Boris's attendance began to drop off.

Boris later made amends for the *Spectator* award by writing a column in the *Telegraph* entitled: "Isn't it time to impeach Blair over Iraq?" – even though Boris himself had supported the war. The *Sunday Times* said: "It is impossible to dislike a man who reverses his opinions on a sixpence, declaring with a harrumphing laugh: 'No, it's total bollocks, isn't it? It's balls.'"

Nor did his constituents feel they were getting a "fair squeeze of the sauce bottle", as Boris put it, until, at the Mayor of Henley's annual dinner, he was hit in the face by a bread roll flung by a Labour councillor. The *Henley Standard* rose to his defence and Boris offered to write a column for them, though they, too, had to put up with his cavalier approach to deadlines.

Again, he knew how to woo the punters.

"If Amsterdam or Leningrad vie for the title of Venice of the North," he wrote, "then Venice – what compliment is high enough?

Venice, with all her civilization and ancient beauty, Venice with her addiction to curious aquatic means of transport, yes, my friends, Venice is the Henley of the South."

Boris and his family were soon sought-after guests at Henley garden parties. He also spearheaded local campaigns but, as always, his time-keeping was not up to scratch. On one occasion he failed to turn up at all as he had been test-driving a Ferrari and had run out of petrol in the fast-lane of the A40 in rush hour, causing a massive tailback.

Sometimes, Petronella Wyatt would be sent in his stead; if he did turn up he would often write his speech on the back of a serviette a few moments before he was due to deliver it, just as he had when visiting girls' schools for debating competitions.

As a constituency residence, he first rented a cottage in Swyncombe. Then in 2003, he bought a £650,000 house in Thame that would be big enough for all the family. The tax payer made a generous contribution through MPs' expenses. A large swimming pool was added; the shelves indoors were filled with improving books. However, given her political views, Marina did not take to living in Henley at all.

When Michael Howard replaced Iain Duncan Smith as leader, he made Boris vice-chairman of the Conservative Party. The whips were against this; Boris was always missing votes on the flimsiest of excuses. Nevertheless, he was quickly promoted to Shadow Arts Minister.

Within minutes of accepting the post, he delivered his off-the-cuff plan to save Britain's arts: "Day one, and I have a six-point programme. I haven't cleared this with anybody, but here is what I think. On coming to power I am going to institute a Windows spell check in English so that schoolchildren in this country no longer feel they have got it wrong when they spell words correctly.

"The Greeks are going to be given an indistinguishable replica of all the Parthenon marbles, done in the most beautiful marble dust to end this acrimonious dispute between our great nations.

"I am going to open up the bandwidth, so there is much more freedom on the radio stations. I am going to reduce some of the stuff allocated to the Pentagon, so you can get the Rolling Stones in Oxfordshire. I am fed up with just listening to treacly old Magic.

"Fourth? I can't remember what point four is. Ah, yes. We are going to convene a summit with Damien Hirst and the rest of the gang at which they are going to explain to the nation what it all means. Let us have a national 'mission to explain' by the Saatchi mob, which will be massively popular.

"We're going to have a national poetry Olympiad to restore rhyme and scansion. There will be some sort of stoop of wine for the winning prize.

"Point six is to move away from Labour's grim, utilitarian approach to culture. I took particular exception to [Education Secretary] Charles Clarke's attack on the classics. If we can't study ancient languages, culture and art, we are deracinating ourselves."

As for Estelle Morris MP, the current Minister for the Arts: "She is a charming lady."

Soon after his appointment, the marketing company Superbrands put Boris on their "cool list", alongside Johnny Depp, Bose stereo and Diesel clothes. The company explained: "… being able to zig, when everybody else zags … there isn't anybody else quite like him. And because he's funny."

Chapter Nine – Bonking Boris

With Boris away in the House, sex scandals were breaking out at the *Spectator*, or *Sextator* as it soon became known. Associate editor Rod Liddle was having an affair with the blonde on reception who was half his age. When his wife found out, she told all to the *Daily Mail*. In the article, she accused Boris of running the "whole place like a knocking shop. It was a case of all being lads together, all girls in short skirts, and 'phwooar, good on yer Rod'."

Next it was discovered that the *Spectator*'s publisher Kimberly Quinn was having an affair with Home Secretary David Blunkett. She had also bedded the Spectator's wine correspondent Simon Hoggart.

While Boris's expected promotion to editor of the *Sunday Telegraph* was again put on hold, Conrad Black found himself the subject of an investigation by the US Securities & Exchange Commission. Hollinger, the parent company for both the *Telegraph* and the *Spectator*, sued Black for $200 million over alleged irregularities and he sold out to the Barclay brothers. Instead of sticking up for his mentor, Boris published a scathing attack on Blake and his wife, while mercilessly lampooning him in private.

Boris was still riding high. His novel *Seventy Two Virgins* had just come out and received a good review from Douglas Hurd – in the *Spectator* it must be said. He said: "I guess that he wrote this in three days, flat out." Hurd also noted that the book mocks every possible attitude to the Iraq War – "which seems in harmony with the official *Spectator* line of supporting the war but impeaching the man who started it".

Parallels between Boris and the book's bike-riding protagonist, Roger Barlow MP, were too good to miss. Boris wrote: "To a man like Roger Barlow, the whole world just seemed to be a complicated joke, an accidental jumble of ingredients on the cosmic stove, which produced our selfish genes. For Barlow, everything was always up for grabs, capable of dispute; and religion, laws, principle, custom – these were nothing by sticks we plucked from the wayside to support our faltering steps."

Even so, Boris was still being tipped for the top job, to which he modestly quipped: "My chances of being PM are about as good as the chances of finding Elvis on Mars, or my being reincarnated as an olive."

In New York's *Vanity Fair* magazine, contributing editor Michael Wolff was comparing him to Ronald Reagan and Arnold Schwarzenegger, though "his state of dishevelment is as great as any I've seen in an employed person". It went on to say that he "has achieved near mythic status in the UK ... While he may more and more often be mentioned as a future Prime Minister, it is always with incredulity".

But bad luck was right around the corner. Having no time to write a leader, Boris called Simon Heffer and asked him to dash one off. The piece was to be about Liverpool's reaction to the death of Ken

Bigley, a Liverpudlian contractor who had been beheaded by Jihadists in Iraq. The city, it said, was "hooked on grief and likes to wallow in a sense of vicarious victimhood".

It went on: "The extreme reaction to Mr Bigley's murder is fed by the fact that he was a Liverpudlian. A combination of economic misfortune … and an excessive predilection for welfarism have created a peculiar and deeply unattractive psyche among many Liverpudlians. They see themselves, whenever possible, as victims and resent their victim status, yet at the same time they wallow in it. Part of this flawed psychological state is that they cannot accept that they might have made any contribution to their misfortunes but seek rather to blame someone else for it."

To add insult to injury, it went on to mention the sensitive topic of the Hillsborough disaster, where 96 Liverpool supporters had died.

"The deaths of more than 50 Liverpool football supporters at Hillsborough in 1989 was undeniably a greater tragedy. But that is no excuse for Liverpool's failure to acknowledge the part played in the disaster by drunken fans. The police became a convenient scapegoat, and the *Sun* a whipping boy for daring to hint at the wider causes."

The *Spectator* was first taken to task for downsizing the death toll from 96 to "more than 50" and an independent panel in 2012 concluded that no Liverpool fans were responsible in any way for the disaster, and that its main cause was a "lack of police control".

The leader was not by-lined, so Boris had to carry the can. What made it worse was that Michael Howard had once been a candidate in Liverpool Edge Hill and was a supporter of Liverpool FC. He dismissed the article as "nonsense from beginning to end", and Boris was duly despatched to Liverpool to apologize in what became known as "Operation Scouse Grovel".

In the eye of the storm, Boris was in his element. He insisted that Michael Howard – or just Howard as he insisted on calling him – was "completely wrong to say that the article was 'nonsense from beginning to end'. I don't think he could have read it properly."

Boris was not into damage limitation. While he admitted that the article presented an "outdated stereotype" and apologized for claiming that drunken Liverpool fans contributed to the Hillsborough disaster, he did not retract the broad thrust of the article.

The moment of truth came when Ken Bigley's brother Paul phoned into a radio station Boris was on to tell him: "You are a self-centred, pompous twit – even your body language on TV is wrong. You don't look right, never mind act right. Get out of public life."

When Boris tried to repeat his apology, Paul Bigley cut him off, saying: "You're waffling again."

On his way out of the studio, he was hijacked by Janet Dacombe whose baby son had been harvested for organs without permission at Liverpool's Alder Hey hospital. She, too, demanded an apology.

"Oh well, that's very interesting," said Boris. "I will report back to Michael Howard and he will write to you."

She insisted on a reply that afternoon.

"Are you trying to save your political career?" yelled a journalist.

"I haven't got a political career," replied Boris. At the end of the day, he said: "I feel like a squeezed lemon on the subject."

Otherwise, Boris came through unscathed. Not only did sales of the *Spectator* increase in the city, it boosted his popularity among fans of Manchester United, Liverpool FC's greatest rivals, dubbing them "self-pity city" and chanting: "There's only one Boris Johnson."

Political commentator and Man U fan Michael Crick said: "This was the first and only time a politician had been celebrated in song." He said there were even Boris badges and leaflets at their Old Trafford ground.

In the end Boris felt he had been forgiven by the people of Liverpool, quipping: "The quality of Mersey is not strained."

The furore had only just died down when rumours surfaced that Boris was having an affair with Petronella Wyatt, the Fleet Street femme fatale who had once conspired to ensnare David Cameron. It had been going on for four years and much of it had been conducted through her "Singular Life" column in the *Spectator* for those who could read between the lines. Sometimes, though, her articles carried a womanly rebuke.

"If a man cannot organize his clothes it is often an indication that he cannot organize much else – either his life or the country," she wrote.

It was a cosy relationship. Petronella even came on a family holiday with Marina and the kids, and there was the irresistible detail of the couple circling her St. John's Wood home in a taxi, snogging on the backseat while the driver played a tape of her singing Puccini.

"Boris doesn't tip much," the cabbie complained.

Even the *Telegraph* cast Boris in the role of the dumb blond in this story, while Boris denied everything with characteristic panache.

"It is complete balderdash," he said. "It is an inverted pyramid of piffle. It is all completely untrue and ludicrous conjecture. I am amazed people can write this drivel."

His use of the word "piffle" delighted those sketch writers who remember his middle name was "de Pfeffel". Despite his protestations, Marina kicked him out in the tweed suit he stood up in. He appeared in the same garb in an otherwise formal do – the Spectator's Parliamentarian of the Year lunch at Claridge's. Both Marina and Petronella were no-shows. Which was as well, as the "Boris problem" was on everyone's lips over the Krug champagne.

Sharing the stage with Michael Howard, Boris spoke of "shrugging off the assaults of the press, which can be less than wholly helpful".

Howard then called the *Spectator* "political Viagra".

"Mr Johnson, listening, froze," wrote columnist Quentin Letts. "His eyes, at that moment, were comparable to the stilled headlamps of a prize turbot on some fishmonger's stall. The mouth assumed a fishy quality, too: gaping, rounded, assembled into an expression of hooked horror."

Mr Howard proceeded to tease his underling, at length. He praised the "terrific enthusiasm" with which Mr Johnson undertook his "various duties".

"You were keen to make your mark on the City of Culture" – Liverpool – "And you succeeded beyond my wildest dreams."

Apparently Boris was not enjoying this.

"Outrageous," he muttered.

"Jacques Cousteau, caught several leagues under the sea, could barely have looked shorter of oxygen," Letts continued.

"Keep it up, Boris!" cried Mr Howard to gales of laughter.

"The audience at a Frankie Howerd film could not have been quicker to seize on the nuances of this phrase," Letts concluded.

Soon Boris was patching it up with Marina, believing that he had lived to fight another day, when Petronella Wyatt's mother told the *News of the World* that her daughter had just had an abortion.

"Of course she told Boris in advance. Apparently he agreed with her decision and his reaction was one of immense relief – just like any other married man caught out by his infidelity," she said.

In the tabloids, "bumbling Boris" and "boisterous Boris" had become "bonking Boris".

Despite being caught out in a lie, Boris refused to quit as Shadow Arts Minister or party vice-chairman. He argued that it was not only justifiable but positively desirable to lie about one's sexual life – citing President Clinton's denial of having sex with Monica Lewinsky.

Michael Howard did not take this view and promptly sacked him. Boris reacted by having a stiff drink, then seizing the opportunity to write about the "surreal joy of being sacked" in the *Telegraph*.

"Nothing excites compassion, in friend and foe alike, as much as the sight of you ker-splonked on the Tarmac with your propeller buried six feet under," he wrote, concluding: "My friends, as I have discovered myself, there are no disasters, only opportunities. And, indeed, opportunities for fresh disasters."

Sympathy over his sacking won Marina around. Their marriage was on the mend and he was soon caught in floral short and skull-and-crossbones ski-hat out on his early morning run from their Islington home – though he returned to find the front door locked and had to wait to be let in.

Despite his long career in journalism, he was less than sanguine about the predations of the paparazzi.

"I saw the bloody photographers outside, so I jumped over the garden wall at the back and eluded them. Then I totally forgot they were there on the way back," he said, When asked why didn't he climb over the wall again rather than stand, locked out, by his front door, he said: "You know when you go for a run, you get rather elated. I sort of had this idea that I would mow them down, like a scene in an old Sylvester Stallone film."

But Boris was not about to mend his ways. In the midst of the storm, he overcame a rare bout of flu and went to speak at an Oxford Union debate at the invitation of Ruzwana Bashir with whom, the press noted, he enjoyed a "close relationship". There were others. Sonia Purnell calls one chapter of her biography, *Just Boris*, "Busting with Spunk", a phase said to have emanated from the lips of the rotund Lothario himself. Elsewhere he boasted of being fuelled by "weapons-grade testosterone".

Nevertheless womenfolk rushed to his aid. Margaret Cook, jilted wife of Foreign Secretary Robin Cook, compared the charms of the Marina's jumpers and Petronella's décolletage. She also pointed out that Marina had ousted Allegra with the age-old ploy of falling pregnant. Even the housewives of Henley on Thames put the blame on Marina – for going out to work.

Male friends warned that, wed to a ferocious lawyer, he might be in for ruinous divorce. Other's blamed Petronella's mother for encouraging her daughter to bag Boris after DC had escaped her grasps. At the *Telegraph* though, editor Charles Moore indulged his star columnist, saying: "I told Boris I don't care about what he does in his private life and he told me, 'Nor do I.'"

Dan Colson also entered in the spirit of the thing, saying: "He always looked like he had just got out of bed and, apparently, he had."

Nobody blamed Boris – least of all Boris. But politically, he had paid the price, though even Michael Howard was soon having second thoughts.

Under the high-minded Catholic Barclay Brothers, things were set to change at the *Spectator*. They installed as chief executive Andrew Neil, who told the BBC: "I think the more time the editor spends in Doughty Street editing the magazine and the less we see of him in the newspapers, then the better for the editor and the better for the magazine."

Ping pong in the garden was banned, along with Ann Sindall's Jack Russell and, presumably, daytime sex.

However, the soap-opera goings-on had only boosted sales of the *Spectator*. Boris was charging £10,000 a time for after-dinner speaking and earning £150,000 a year from TV and other journalism. This was on top of his £59,000 MP's salary and the undisclosed sum he got for editing the *Spectator*. He could even have afforded a new suit.

Neil promised a "period of quiet" at the *Spectator*. Instead, the BBC aired the *Spectator Affair*, a behind-the-scenes look at the workings of the magazine. Fearing that he would be asked about his personal life, Boris, at first, avoided appearing. Then, when it seemed that others were co-operating, he deigned to give an on-camera interview.

His inquisitor said: "I have never seen anyone who is tougher behind the eyes than him in a billion years of interviewing ... He is a charmingly evasive ruthless customer."

Though the peccadillos of Rod Liddle and Kimberly Quinn were given an airing, Petronella was airbrushed – leading to accusations that Boris had done a deal over access with the producers.

Conrad Black appeared, saying: "Boris had his charms, but Boris is not Mr Loyalty."

Behind closed doors, Boris blamed Black for his downfall. However, they made it up and Boris wrote a supportive letter to the judge in Chicago when Black came to trial.

When it came to the election in 2005, Boris was kept in check – even though he was potentially a vote winner. His one contribution to the campaign was an update of his old *GQ* joke, which was now rendered: "Voting Tory will cause your wife to have bigger breasts and increase your chances of owning a BMW M3."

The only place he was to be seen was in Teignbridge, South Devon, where Stanley was a candidate. He lost out to the Lib-Dems. The Conservatives barely put a dent in Labour's stranglehold on parliament, but Boris increased his majority in Henley, though he was nowhere to be seen.

After that, he withdrew from constituency politics. He had bigger concerns in town. *Spectator* staffers Lloyd Evans and Toby Young put on the play *Who's the Daddy?* at the King's Head Theatre in Islington, satirizing the bonkathon at the magazine. Other staffers packed the audience.

"I don't know whether I'll have time to catch it before it closes," Boris told the press. "I'm certainly issuing no instructions to staff about it. It will not be deemed an act of disloyalty to go and see it."

The authors had warned him of its content. He replied, resignedly: "I always had a feeling that my life would turn into a farce."

They even borrowed this line for the play where Boris's character says: "Fine – turn my life into a farce, everyone else has."

Questioned about the play in the *Independent*, he said he felt "eirenic" – peace-seeking – and "ataraxic" – serenely calm.

"I was due for a good kicking," he admitted.

He could have sacked Evans and Young, but showed them the indulgence others had shown him. In response, they turned down the offer of a transfer to the West End.

Marina stood by him, turning out for the annual *Spectator* summer party. But Boris said any day he expected to join the "Valhalla of ex-*Spectator* editors". Meanwhile the atmosphere at the office had become one of "monastic seclusion and contemplation".

"I can't quite remember what happens in *The Name of the Rose*," he said. "Oh, it gets rather racy, doesn't it? OK, forget it."

Chapter Ten – Eton Rules

After losing the 2005 election, Michael Howard stepped down as Tory leader. Asked whether he would stand for the position, Boris said: "My hat is firmly in the sock draw, where it will remain."

Instead he supported fellow OE David Cameron against the "Stain" David Davis, who then was favourite.

"I'm backing David Cameron's campaign out of pure, cynical self-interest," Boris said. With his backing, Cameron's odds shortened considerably.

Cameron won the leadership. Nevertheless, Boris plainly thought the job was rightfully his and, in his *Telegraph* column, damned Cameron with faint praise.

"Over the past few months I have lost count of the number of people who have asked me – satirically – why I am not standing in the current Tory leadership contest; and after I have bumbled out some reply, they have always said, oh well, who are you backing? 'David Cameron,' I have said, quick as a flash, and for the most part this answer has so far drawn a look of anxious blankness, the look you see when people are sure that they ought to have read some classic work, and are in two minds whether to bluff it out or admit ignorance. 'Oh yes,' they say, mentally noting that they ought to get to grips with the subject of David Cameron, along with Stephen

Hawking's *Brief History of Time* and *Midnight's Children* by Salman Rushdie ..."

Though Boris was a supporter, he said: "You may not want to go quite as far as Bruce Anderson, whose essay on Cameron in this week's *Spectator* is a kind of tear-sodden *nunc dimittis*. Like old Simeon in the temple, Brucie has seen our salvation ... though you may not be prepared to agree with him that Cameron is our saviour and a light to lighten the gentiles, and the glory of the Tory party ..."

What's more Cameron was a young whipper-snapper. But the forty-one-year-old Boris conceded "it has been the 38-year-old's week".

The problem was that Cameron was just a pale imitation of the real deal.

"... I like this stuff about there being a 'we as well as a me' in politics. I like his constant repetition of 'we're all in this together'; indeed, I am vain enough to have a feeling that he nicked it from me."

He concluded: "... the Tories must rediscover compassionate Conservative ... That is the job for Cameron, and Cameron is the man for the job." A neat phrase, perhaps, but it sounds like empty sloganeering.

Boris had yet to choose between journalism and politics. On *Desert Island Discs*, Sue Lawley pushed him on the point. He flannelled, but was forced to come down on the side of politics. Then she got him to pitch for a job on David Cameron's front bench. What of his own ambitions for leadership? she went on. Boris had to admit: "I suppose all politicians in the end are like crazed wasps in a jam jar, each individually convinced they are going to make it … My silicon chip, my ambition silicon chip, has been programmed to try to scrabble my way up this *curus honorum*, this ladder of things …"

Like most other people, Boris had spent years writing and revising his list of eight records. In the event, when he handed over his selection, the producer sucked her teeth.

"Your choices … it's just that they seem so political," she said. "It's like you're kind of trying to appeal to everyone, a bit of Stones, a bit of Bach, you know. I mean, Nigella Lawson chose Eminem!"

His other choices were the Beatles, Van Morrison, Hadyn, The Clash, Beethoven and the theme tune from *Test Match Special*.

"I was shattered, and insulted to the core," Boris wrote in the *New Statesman*. "'But I love this music. And, much as I like him, I don't want Eminem on a desert island.' She then tried to reassure me about my taste, and what exquisite choices they were, but I couldn't help feeling, as she left, that I had failed one of life's great tests."

With a nod from Boris, Frank Johnson wrote an imaginary conversion between David Cameron and George Osborne which was published in the *Spectator*.

Mr Cameron: 'Anything else we need worry about, George?'

Mr Osborne: 'Well, yeah. Boris has just announced on Desert Island Discs that he's going into politics.'

Mr Cameron: 'What? Why isn't he content to be MP for Henley?'

Mr Osborne: 'He said he thought it will soon be time for him to choose. So if we win, he says he'd like to be a front-bench spokesman for agriculture or trade or something like that.'

Mr Cameron: 'You mean, he intends to join our front bench?'

Mr Osborne: 'Looks like it. What are we gonna do?'

Mr Cameron: 'Well, I shall say that I think he has taken a brave and correct decision in the interests of country and party, and that I wish him well in whatever he turns his considerable talents to next, and that none of this is any reflection on his ability.'

Mr Osborne: 'No, Dave. That's what you say when he has to resign from the front bench again, not when he joins it again.'

Mr Cameron: 'Oh, yes. I was jumping ahead a bit.'

As it was, when Cameron announced his Shadow Cabinet, Boris wasn't in it. The next day, he was appointed Shadow Minister for Higher Education and he was forced to give up the editorship of the *Spectator*. Cameron was not about to risk another Liverpool.

Instead, Boris gave him a Portsmouth, calling it a city "too full of drugs, obesity, underachievement and Labour MPs". Then he managed to offend a whole country, saying the Tory party had "become used to Papua New Guinea-style orgies of cannibalism and chief-killing". When the High Commissioner demanded an apology, Boris said: "Add Papua New Guinea to my global itinerary of apologies."

At the *Times Higher Education Supplement*, political correspondent Anna Fazakerley greeted his appointment with glee. "Rumple and ready to rumble" the headline said. However, Boris stepped back from his early promise to slash "looney degrees in windsurfing at Bangor University". He now said: "My instincts are not to go around trying to exterminate Mickey Mouse courses. One man's Mickey Mouse course is another's *literae humanitores.*"

Bolstered by his stand in higher education, Boris stood for the position of rector of Edinburgh University – a position previously held by Gladstone, Gordon Brown and his hero Churchill. This gave him an opportunity to chat up students in short skirts and he got to sign one student's bare chest. However, there was an "Anyone But Boris" campaign with the slogan "Practice safe X – don't wake up with a dumb blond".

In the vote, he came third to a Green member of the Scottish Parliament and the editor of the *Scotsman*, a fellow OE.

Relieved of his duties at the *Spectator*, Boris found time hanging heavy on his hands, so he made a two part series for BBC Two called *Dream of Rome.* In it, he sought to discover how the ancient Romans managed to run a united empire, while the European Union could not.

He wrote a book to accompany the series and was heard complaining "bloody hard work, this book thing". Asked how long it had taken him, he replied: "Bloody hell, two weeks."

In anyone else's hands this might have been dull, but to Boris the Barbarians were "clad in nothing but the kind of fur accessories you might find in a fetish shop – a seal-skin jockstrap, a rabbit-skin loincloth" and their wives would "bare their breasts in a kind of *Sun* Page 3 exhortation to the troops".

He made a follow-up TV series called *After Rome*: *Holy War and Conquest*. This got him into trouble with the parliamentary authorities as he had not declared his shareholding in the production company. He also upped his fee for his weekly column on the *Telegraph* and was bringing in over half-a-million pounds a year.

The topic for his column would come from a session with his parliamentary staff. Then a staffer would do the research. This did not take long as Boris insisted there should be no more than three facts per article. Then he would knock the whole thing out in ninety minutes. For each column he got £5,000.

He would also encourage staffers compete to come up with topics that would cause the most catastrophic consequences for his career, such as "Why I believe in a European superstate". Boris's favourite was "Why David Cameron is a complete c**t". He even got round to writing the intro.

His opinions were never less than forthright. Interviewed for the Christian magazine *Third Way*, he expressed pride in his "mongrel" background and his Muslim, Jewish and Christian heritage. Indeed, his children were a quarter Indian. And he told Muslim students that they should inter-marry – "then all our problems would go away".

After less than four months in office, Bonking Boris was at it again. This time, the *News of the World* caught him sneaking in and out of Anna Fazackerley's Chelsea flat. They may have been discussing higher education, but why was Boris so furtive and why did he find it necessary to cover his distinctive hair with a beanie hat? They were seen out together and one source said: "They also got overheated in the back of a cab and were told to 'cool it' by the driver taking them to a function."

On one occasion, after two hours with Anna, the *News of the World* said Boris emerged sheepishly and took a taxi to Petronella's place in St John's Wood where he stayed for another couple of hours before returning home to Marina.

When the paper approached Boris to give them a quote, he said: "You're very kind. But no thank you. Absolutely not. No comment whatsoever. Thanks a lot. Bye."

As a result of the article, Anna had to duck out of covering his fact-finding tour of China. While he was away, Marina lodged a protest with the Press Complaints Commission when journalists besieged their Islington home. She moved her wedding ring to her middle figure and the children were farmed out to a friend in the country. But after Boris returned from China, he took Marina away on a family holiday and the press coverage died down.

Cameron took no action, while on his website, Boris said: "Heads down and tin hats on while news stories fly." His secretary added: "Boris's talent and ability can weather any storm."

Certainly being branded a philanderer in the tabloids had not dented his popularity. When he was asked to play in a charity football match against Germany, the crowd cried: "We want Boris."

He took his higher-education brief very seriously, visiting universities around the country – though often turning up in impossibly flashy cars, courtesy of his *GQ* motoring column. He would be in his parliamentary office until nine or ten at night, writing speeches and would often work over the weekends. There were, as always, the prolonged absences though, and his boss, Shadow Education Secretary David Willetts, found it difficult to work with a junior who had a higher political profile that his.

Boris managed to upstage Cameron's first Conservative Party Conference speech in 2006, by taking a swipe at Jamie Oliver who was promoting healthy eating in schools. At a fringe meeting Boris stood up for mothers who smuggled fast food to the children through school fences.

"I say let people eat what they like," he said. "Why shouldn't they push pies through the railings? If I was in charge, I would get rid of Jamie Oliver."

To still the maelstrom, Boris was forced to back down, saying: "I was completely misquoted. Jamie Oliver is a saint," later calling him "the Messiah".

Putting a brave face on it, Cameron said: "It's been a great week – even Boris made it until Tuesday afternoon before he put his foot in it."

While critics were saying that Boris could not be taken seriously, they suddenly took him very seriously when he said in the *Telegraph* that Iran should be assisted to build an atomic bomb – which it would eventually build anyway – in return for assurances that it would not attack Israel and make progress towards democracy. It was a line he had pushed early. It was rumoured that Boris's planned elevation to Shadow Minister for Europe was scuppered by this piece. Boris, it was concluded, was still more interested in journalism than politics.

Further humiliation came when Michael Gove, one of Boris's stooges at Oxford and three years his junior, was installed as his boss. The entire Shadow Cabinet was now younger than him.

At the time, the Tories were having difficulties finding a candidate to stand for Mayor of London against Labour's incumbent Ken Livingstone. At one point, they had even discussed fielding a joint Conservative-Lib Dem candidate in Greg Dyke, but he pulled out.

Polling data indicated that Livingstone could be defeated and Veronica Wadley, editor the London *Evening Standard*, let it be known that she would support Boris. Denied advancement inside parliament, Boris realized that the only way he could make it to the top was to establish a power base outside it.

News that he intended to stand was leaked in bumbling fashion by Boris, by accident, when he bumped in to the BBC political editor Nick Robinson, who he had known at university, on the tube. But neither Robinson – nor any of the people he told – believed it was true.

Boris then denied that he was going to stand. Then he admitted that being Mayor of London was a "fantastic job" and that a lot of people were urging him to run, but he did not want to give up his Henley constituency, along with his parliamentary salary and expenses.

A compromise was reached. This allowed him to keep his constituency until the mayoral election. But he gave up his Shadow Higher Education brief immediately and got his nomination in for

Mayor just hours before the deadline. The party leadership still had cold feet, but they had no other credible candidate.

Boris outside parliament was not under their control. On the other hand, with his flair for publicity, he did not need their endorsement. Boris romped through the newly instituted primaries. Then came the main event – Boris versus Ken.

Livingstone admitted that Boris was the most formidable opponent he had faced, but that being Mayor was not a job for a celebrity. Running a huge city was a serious business. Ken had a good track record in the job, modernizing transport and, on his watch, London had overtaken New York as the world's financial centre. Against that Boris had a rocky parliamentary career and a couple of sex scandals to his name.

What's more, Gordon Brown had just taken over as Prime Minister and Labour were having a honeymoon. Boris also had a millstone. In twenty years of journalism, he had committed his thoughts to paper. With a skilled set of scissors, it was possible to make him look like a racist, a homophobe, a right-wing bigot and a toff totally out of touch with the needs of a modern multicultural city like London. Ken was a Londoner, born and bred, while Boris had no natural affinity for the city.

Nevertheless with The Clash blaring out "London Calling", Boris launched his campaign. His one policy announcement was the abolition of the bendy bus and the return of the sturdy double-decker. While he was serious about becoming Mayor, he said, he reserved the right to make jokes.

"Are you too funny to be Mayor?" asked a reporter from the *Wall Street Journal*.

He was a hero to the party faithful at the Conservative conference that year, though the governor of California's comments had him dubbed "The Fumbulator" on the internet. Still, the publicity did him no harm.

The Conservative Party's position was strengthened when Brown "bottled it" that summer and decided not to go for an early election. This was a relief for Boris who would have fought in Henley again as well as running for Mayor. He had enough on his plate. On top of his constituency work, there were still his weekly column for the *Telegraph*, his television commitments and a new book to promote. Many assumed that he was not actually out to win mayoralty, believing that a credible defeat would give his political standing enough of a boost.

He had a small campaign team ensconced in Centre Point over a mile-and-a-half from Tory headquarters in Millbank Tower. They had little experience and were up against Livingstone's Labour Party machine that outnumbered them by thirty to one. Boris depended on his fame and charisma to do the job.

The Tory top brass lent him some staff, but it was soon clear that his campaign was a shambles. It was only then that the Conservatives realised that, if they could not take London, it would harm their chances in the next general election.

Boris, as always, got lucky. In the *Evening Standard*, Andrew Gilligan accused Lee Jasper, Livingstone's director of policing and equalities, of cronyism and corruption. He was later cleared, but the story tarnished the reputation of the Labour regime.

The campaign headquarters was moved to the old County Hall building across the river from parliament, so Boris could be reined in, and the former treasurer of the Conservative Party Lord Marland was sent in with a war chest of £1.5 million.

Next Lynton Crosby, the "Wizard of Oz" who had won four elections of John Howard in Australia, was brought in. He did not come cheap. When Crosby and Marland invited him to lunch, Boris knew what was coming. He first thing he told them was that he had already booked an appointment for a haircut. They told him that losing was not an option and if he let them down – "we'll cut your fucking knees off".

Another Australian, James McGrath, was called in to apply military discipline. With his hair cut and combed, Boris was kitted out with smart suits, shirts and ties. A third antipodean was employed to give Boris media training. His bumbling may have been all right on *Have I Got News For You?* but now he need to speak in sound bites.

Although Boris found his minders "scary", research had shown them that Boris had a likeability factor that eclipsed the other candidates, even with people who did not share his political opinions. While Livingstone was a leftist ideologue inhabiting Zone One and Two, Boris was somehow apolitical, speaking up for the concerns of ordinary Londoners rather than playing politics. Boris's team targeted the outer suburbs where people were more likely to vote Tory, but had not voted in previous mayoral elections. In response, Labour wheeled out its political big guns. But the more they demonized Boris as "some sort of right-wing Neanderthal", the better he looked. No one could be as bad as they said.

Crosby then made Boris "green", despite his previous assaults on the tree-hugging brigade. This was a rerun of his campaign to be president of the Oxford Union – he would be everything to everyone.

Boris was still widely perceived as clueless, while Livingstone had been in office for eight years. But Ken was past his sell-by date and BoJo, as he was then dubbed, was seen as the coming man.

Then Marina put her shoulder to the wheel, going on walkabouts with Boris, sometimes with David and Samantha Cameron. She was a well-known leftie and her appearance by his side made it seem that even she had been won over.

In the first televised debate with Ken and the Lib-Dem candidate Brian Paddick, Boris got the better of it by raising the recent spate of teenage murders.

"It breaks my heart to see so many kids growing up scared, and so many adults scared of kids," he said. No sign of the joking, bumbling Boris of old there.

When Labour Home Secretary Jacqui Smith said that she was frightened to go out for a kebab in her area of Peckham, Boris declared: "I want London to be safe for Jacqui Smith … I want the most dangerous thing in Peckham to be the kebab itself."

Crime became Boris's lead policy of the campaign – on the journalistic grounds that "if it bleeds, it leads," Livingstone said.

However, abolishing the bendy buses came back to bite Boris. He said that the cost of employing conductors on the fleet of new Routemasters would be just £8 million a year. It would be more, as more Routemasters would be needed.

Boris was soon said to be "fuming" that the police were pursuing him for the theft of Tariq Aziz's cigar case, which Boris had taken from the bombed-out ruins of Saddam Hussein's Deputy Prime Minister's home. He had admitted as much in his *Telegraph* column five years earlier. He was forced to hand it over four months later, but by then he was Mayor of London.

At the time, he protested that Scotland Yard should be concentrating on knife crime, rather than harassing him over a little souvenir collecting. As luck would have it, the matter was eclipsed by fresh allegations of sleaze against Lee Jasper – this time that he was having an undeclared relationship with a woman who received funding from City Hall. He was forced to resign, though the police found that there was no criminal case to answer.

With Livingstone on the back foot, Boris attacked the overseas offices – or Kenbassies – he had set up and the "ludicrous Pyonyang-style newspaper" City Hall produced. *The Times* then discovered that Livingstone was planning to extend the congestion-charge zone. Boris went on the offensive in the areas concerned, dubbing Ken Livingstone "Ken Leaving-soon". A disastrous budget then caused Labour to slump in the polls.

GQ demonstrated its loyalty by ranking Boris the fourteenth worst dressed British male; Ken came in at number eleven. *The Times* then carried the story that while Gordon Brown had all but written off Livingstone's chances, allies were consoling themselves that a victory for Boris "would be a disaster" for Cameron. To counter this, Cameron turned out alongside Boris at a meeting in Edmonton with black youth leader Ray Lewis, now a regular companion of Boris on the campaign trail.

Boris was, Cameron said, "a man who is as big a figure as Ken Livingstone – and twice as charismatic; a man who is just as determined as Ken Livingstone – and twice as energetic ... I don't always agree with him but I respect the fact that he's absolutely his own man. He's a proper Conservative."

Labour's deputy leader Harriet Harman gave Boris's crime agenda another unwitting boost when she donned a stab-proof vest for a tour of her Peckham constituency with the police. However, he was not helped when the BNP endorsed him on their website. Several black City Hall workers told the *Voice* that they were genuinely afraid of what would happen to them if Boris was elected. But Boris was not the monster portrayed by Livingstone's campaign. People saw that for themselves because of his appearances on *Have I Got News For You?* However, Boris's campaign team had similar worries, fearing that the *Evening Standard*'s unrelenting support might prove counterproductive.

Boris's sexual history did not count against him either when it came out that Ken had five children with three different women. This was not secret, merely private, Ken said: "I don't think anybody in this city is shocked about what consenting adults do."

So nothing was made of "Bonking Boris" during the campaign. On this matter, the two men called a gentlemanly truce. However, there were some ructions when *Marie Claire* published an interview where Boris admitted to smoking dope before going up to Oxford and saying that he might have taken cocaine while he was there.

Labour ministers and MPs were banned from calling Boris by his first name. He was to be called "Boris Johnson" or "the Conservative candidate". "Boris" made him sound too cuddly. So Boris stopped referring to Livingstone as "Ken", calling him rather "the Labour mayor".

Former Tory MP George Walden urged Londoners not to vote, saying of Boris: "... the most entertaining thing about Johnson is when he puts on his serious, solicitous look. Like David Cameron, he is coming to believe in his own sincerity. Servility to celebrity has partially replaced class deference, and the adoring polls suggest that Johnson benefits from both. A Greek grocer I knew put his finger on it. Musing about how Alan Clark imagined relieving himself on the public from his ministerial balcony, he concluded: 'The English don't mind being pissed on, so long as it's from a great height.'"

While Boris had backtracked from the £8 million for conductors on Routemasters, he was skewered by Jeremy Paxman on *Newsnight* who asked him thirteen times for a more realistic figure. Later he was caught privately admitting that the figure would be closer to £100 million. But being slapped down by Paxman somehow made Boris all the more endearing and, in the TV debates, even Ken was seen to laugh at his jokes.

At a public meeting in Westminster, Boris broke with the party line and called for an amnesty for illegal immigrants. This sank accusations that he was a racist once and for all. With his Turkish heritage and quarter-Indian children, Boris told the interviewer on the BBC Asian Network: "You can't out-ethnic me."

At a meeting of the gay-rights lobby Stonewall, he was asked whether he could "out-gay the gays" by revealing whether, perhaps at Eton, he had had some gay sexual experience. After a pause, Boris said: "Er ... not so far."

Asked on the *Politics Show* to sum up the other two candidates in one word, Brian Paddick said: "Tragedy; comedy."

With a week to go, Cameron's advisors were already discussing how to protect their leader should anything go wrong when Boris was in office. Boris was already telling the viewers of *Question Time*: "I would gladly embarrass any government that is in power, if it was in the interests of Londoners."

While Ken was practically conceding defeat in the press, Boris's friends were still wielding the knife. On the eve of polling, Simon Heffer wrote in the *Telegraph*: "Mr Johnson is not a politician. He is an act ... The act is calculated and it has required serious application and timing of the sort of which only a clever man is capable. For some of us the joke has worn not thin, but out ... It conceals two things: a blinding lack of attention to detail, and (though this might seem to sit ill with the first point) a ruthless ambition ... The guiding theme of his life is the charm of doing nothing properly. His sins themselves are charming in that they are the sort of failings that upset the Edwardians, and few others since. He is pushy, he is thoughtless, he is indiscreet about his private life. None of this matters much to anyone these days, which is why he has gone so far in spite of them, and tomorrow may go further still."

On the morning of the poll itself, the *Guardian* ran five pages of blistering personal attacks on Boris, under the headline: "Be Afraid, Be Very Afraid."

The following day, their worst nightmare came true.

Chapter Eleven – Boss Boris

More than a million people had voted for Boris, giving him a fifty-thousand lead over Ken on the first count. When the second preference votes were counted, Boris's lead increased to 140,000. Ken said that Boris bounced over to him and said: "This is all Gordon Brown's fault."

Boris's success astounded even him. He was the first Conservative to hold executive power in eleven years and he had the biggest personal mandate of any politician in the country, the third biggest in Europe behind the presidents of Russia and France.

He made a gracious acceptance speech without a hint of triumphalism, thanking particularly Ken Livingstone for shaping the office of Mayor and his service to London. Echoing Mrs Thatcher's quoting of St Francis of Assisi, he said: "We have a new team ready to go into City Hall. Where there have been mistakes we will rectify them. Where there are achievements we will build on them. Where there are neglected opportunities we will seize on them … Let's get cracking tomorrow and let's have a drink tonight."

Later, he aped Tony Blair's New Labour pledge with: "I was elected as new Boris and I will govern as new Boris."

Then it was off to Millbank Tower where they were entertained by an all-girl blonde band and Cameron, awkwardly, held Boris's hand aloft as the winner. Cameron later quipped that Boris would not let go – it was "like the first gay marriage".

The following day he attended the signing-in ceremony in a plain dark suit and white shirt, where four hundred supporters chanted: "Bor-ris! Bor-ris!" He then tripped over and complained that the stage had been booby-trapped. Afterwards, he warned any dogs in the manger that he would have them humanely euthanized.

He would take over the seals of office the following day.

"Until that time," he said. "I imagine there are shredding machines quietly puffing and panting away in various parts of the building, and quite right too. Heaven knows what we shall uncover in the course of the next few days."

When he took over at City Hall, Boris shook the hands of the six-hundred staff. Unlike Ken, he did not bring a team with him and only slowly began making his own appointments. Ann Sindall was brought in from the *Spectator*. Guto Harri, a friend from Oxford, became director of communications, having previously turned down a similar post with Cameron. Ray Lewis became Deputy Mayor for Young People.

Cameron loyalist Nick Boles was installed as acting chief of staff by Central Office, leading Boris to suspect he was a spy. Indeed, he reported back that Boris seemed ill-prepared for office. Meanwhile Rachel went on *Question Time* and promised Londoner's years of "Boris-induced sunshine". His victory, she said, had given the Tory party "a collective orgasm".

A week after becoming mayor, Boris bade farewell to his parliamentary constituency with a letter to the *Henley Standard* that read: "When I set out on my mission to unseat Ken Livingstone more than nine months ago, there were all kinds of risks. There was a considerable risk that I would be thrashed by the Great Newt. And then there was a risk that I would win – and therefore lose Henley, just about the loveliest seat in the House of Commons. At the time, I have to admit, it seemed a pretty small risk…"

It was clear to some that Boris did not even want the mayoralty. He told Brian Paddick that he was "very concerned he was going to win because of the money". The salary, at £143,911, was more than the Prime Minister's, but he had around £100,000 a year in school fees to pay. He feared that he would have to give up his column on the *Telegraph*, but the paper found him too valuable to let go. To deflect criticism, Boles insisted that he donate a fifth of his fee to charity.

"It's outrageous," he said. "I've been raped."

Nevertheless he had to concede the "Boles tax". However, he managed to trim the twenty percent down to around seven. It would be used to support students of journalism and pay for Classics courses in state schools.

Senior editors at the *Telegraph* were assigned to baby-sit his column and steer him away from any potentially explosive topics, though Boris feared this might quench his natural exuberance. Even so, disregarding copyright, he would also publish his columns on his own website before they came out in the paper, often giving him extra coverage in the media.

Boris basked in his new stardom, doing the round of social events. The *Tatler* said: "The priapic Bozza is pure party Viagra."

He even made up with the *Guardian*, telling them: "Every day I wake up in a state of wonderment that I have been elected – obviously knowing that millions of other people wake up in a state of wonderment that I have been elected too."

There were the pitfalls of office to deal with too. Ray Lewis had to go when it was discovered that his CV was not all he said it was and James McGrath, who had worked on Boris's campaign countering accusations of racism, was summarily fired after he said something that could have been interpreted as racist.

When it was clear that Boris, on his own admission, did not "have the faintest clue" what he was doing, Simon Milton, leader of Westminster Council, was called into play the Stuart Reid role. Alongside him would be Tim Parker, whose job-slashing in industry had earned him the nickname "the Prince of Darkness". But when it was clear that Boris could not just be a figurehead as he planned, Parker had to go too.

To demonstrate his political virility, Boris took a swing at Cameron in the *Telegraph*, saying that Britain's sporting triumphs at the Beijing Olympics show that it was "piffle" to claim that we had a "broken society" as the party leader had said. Then Boris set off to wave the flag at the closing ceremony in Beijing looking like a human laundry basket.

Among the old staffers at City Hall, few heads rolled. They were not a bunch of Marxists as Boris had been told and most were happy to stay on. One of their few complaints was that Boris did not take a shower after cycling to work and the windows of City Hall – which Boris dubbed "the testicle" – were not designed to open. Deodorant was recommended.

Boris set about ousting Metropolitan Police Commissioner Sir Ian Blair, who was still embroiled in the fallout from the shooting of Jean Charles de Menezes. Though he did not actually have the power to sack him, Boris assumed the role of Brutus. Blair resigned, saying: "Without the Mayor's backing I do not think I can continue." Policing continued to cause problems throughout his administration, but after the departure of Blair, Boris judiciously stepped down as chairman of the Metropolitan Police Authority.

After a year in office, a poll in the *Evening Standard* gave Boris a ringing endorsement. The *Economist* said: "It may be that a bold personality and cautious policies are the right mix for a London mayor."

He suffered little criticism in the press as he had worked alongside most of the editors. Even Jeremy Paxman was a family friend. What's more, he could take credit for Crossrail and the preparations for the 2012 Olympics both set in motion during Ken Livingstone's watch. The only criticism that hit home was that Boris was now boring. Nevertheless, *Time* magazine named him one of the world's hundred most influential people – a list devoid of the name Cameron, who Boris continued to snipe at tangentially from the columns of the *Telegraph*.

Boris found that he was well out of the House of Commons when the expenses scandal struck in May 2009. David Cameron had to pay back nearly £1,000 after charging for having wisteria removed from a chimney, while Gordon Brown had to repay £12,400. Boris claimed to be amazed at the expense claims of his former colleagues.

"I'm almost embarrassed that I seem to have completely failed to claim for all these things that my colleagues claimed," he said. "Unless you're completely insane or devious or a Liberal Democrat, then there is no way you can fiddle your bike expenses."

As it was the *Telegraph* who was spilling the beans of MPs' expenses, he was on the inside track. It turned out that he claimed – legitimately – £85,299 for mortgage payments on his constituency home, plus £16.50 for a Remembrance Sunday wreath. This had been an oversight, he said, which he happily repaid.

However, as the net spread wider, a deputy mayor was caught fiddling his expenses. Bicycling Boris himself had run up a bill of £4,698 in taxis during his first year in office.

"Where exactly does Boris cycle?" asked one blogger. "Is it just to and from photo shoots?"

At the time, Boris was being photographed a lot on his bike when the tube drivers went out on strike. Boris and his bike became a symbol of Londoners carrying on regardless.

Becoming mayor had not hurt Boris's earning power as he had feared. The family moved into a £2.3-million Georgian townhouse overlooking Regent's Canal. In contravention of planning regulations, he erected a shed on the back balcony. The local council made him take it down. When LBC's Nick Ferrari asked him about it, Boris accused him of "intruding in the private grief" of a man now sadly "ex-shed".

On the trip to New York to visit Mayor Michael Bloomberg, Boris found Americans lining up in Times Square to shake his hand. Back in London, he took a cameo role in *EastEnders*, playing himself, though he has never seen the show – or, for that matter, *Coronation Street*.

At the party conference in the run-up to the 2010 General Election, Boris managed to upstage both David Cameron and William Hague, playing the well-worn Eurosceptic card and wooing the crowd with the line: "It's wonderful to be here in Manchester – one of the few great British cities I have yet to insult."

Cameron was furious.

Boris went on to stick up for bankers. They had, after all, backed his mayoral campaign.

As mayor, the Tory party could not hold him under its thrall. He treated House of Commons committees with contempt and Mayor's Question Time in front of the twenty-five members of the London Assembly as a game. He would dodge questions and hurl carefully crafted insults at his inquisitors.

Chapter Twelve – Call for Boris

When the general election was called in 2010, Boris predicted a majority of forty for David Cameron. He stepped in to help his brother Jo, who was running in Orpington, and generously donated a few *bon mots*. He called Gordon Brown a "holepunch-hurling horror" and Nick Clegg "a cutprice edition of David Cameron hastily knocked off by a Shanghai sweatshop to satisfy unexpected market demand".

When Cameron failed to win a majority, Rachel Johnson tweeted: "It's all gone tits up. Time to call for Boris."

In the end though, with the help of Nick Clegg, Cameron took the keys to Number Ten. This changed everything for Boris. In his skilfully crafted plan, he had intended only to serve one term as mayor, then return to Westminster as the party's saviour.

While Boris pondered his future, news broke that City Hall art adviser Helen Macintyre had a blonde-haired child. She was a brunette. So was her long-term partner, Canadian financier Pierre Rolin, who Macintyre had persuaded to pay £80,000 towards Boris's "Olympian Erection" – the 400-foot red metal ArcelorMittal Orbit tower at the Olympic Park. Soon after, she moved out of his £5-million property. Boris neither confirmed nor denied that the child was his.

A source close to Johnson said: "It's quite likely he hasn't the faintest idea."

Rolin was not invited to the Olympic games. Nor did he get his money back.

Once more Marina removed her wedding ring and threw him out of the house. And once again she took him back again. Everything was patched up with a two-week family holiday in Tanzania, though Boris got swept away by the strong current in the Zanzibar Channel and had to be rescued. After another trip, to India, he was allowed to return home.

The resort they stayed at cost over £700 a night. This was in the age of Osborne austerity. Boris got away with even this without comment.

Osborne tried to clip his wings by slashing London's budget. Boris thwarted this by leaping to the defence of Crossrail, though he knew it was not under threat. On another occasion, when negotiating new powers for the mayor, Boris launched himself over the table to grab Cameron's briefing papers, resulting in an unseemly tug of war.

Before he had left office, Ken Livingstone had suggested a scheme of street-corner bike hire across the city. These became Boris bikes and he was happy to take credit for them at the 2012 election. "Borismaster" buses hit the streets and, the champion of small government, committed public money to build a cable car over the river between the Royal Docks at the O2 Arena. He also backed the building of "Boris Island" in the Thames Estuary to house a new international airport.

When the government proposed a £400-a-week cap on housing benefit, which would force poorer people out of central London, Boris went on air and said: "What we will not accept is any kind of Kosovo-style social cleansing of London."

And he continued to use his *Telegraph* column and appearances on *Question Time* to take pot shots at Cameron's policies. Perhaps not wanting him back in the House of Commons, Cameron invited Boris and Marina to dinner at Number Ten, letting it be known that he was four-square behind Boris's re-election as mayor. Once again he would take on Ken.

When the phone-hacking scandal broke, Boris hastily cancelled a family outing to a Take That concert as guests of Rebekah Brooks and let Cameron take the flak.

During the riots of 2011, Boris was in a Winnebago in the Rockies with Marina and the kids. Boris did not return. This bore a poor comparison to Ken Livingstone who flew back on the first plane from Singapore, where he was lobbying for the Olympics, after the 7/7 bombings in 2005.

But when Theresa May and David Cameron broke off their holidays, Boris's hand was forced to catch a flight home. Beating them to the punch, he filed a piece for the *Evening Standard* on the way. Nevertheless, in riot-torn areas, he was greeted with jeers.

Then suddenly, he was seen with a broom, ready to lead the clean-up of the streets, and the jeers turned to cheers. He dined with David Cameron that night. The following morning, on the *Today* programme, he blamed the riots on the government for cutting police numbers.

Boris then turned up thirty minutes late for a meeting of COBRA, the national emergency committee. Cameron was incandescent.

He was in trouble again when Sir Michael Scholar, chairman of the UK Statistics Authority said that Boris had given misleading figures to the House of Commons Home Affairs Select Committee. Boris dismissed Scholar as a "Labour stooge".

Boris claimed that serious youth crime was coming down, when in fact stabbings were going up, and that police numbers were going up, when in the Metropolitan area they were going down. However, he scored highly in the law-and-order debate in 2009, intervening personally in a mugging when documentary film maker and Ken Livingstone supporter Franny Armstrong was pushed against a car by a group of young girls, one wielding an iron bar. Boris, who was cycling past, picked up the iron bar and cycled after the girls calling them "oiks". Armstrong described Boris as her "knight on a shining bicycle".

London's budget was in difficulties – not least because of the money spent on buying land for the Olympics – but that did not stop Boris pumping money into the outer borough that had won him the election in 2008. Trailing Ken in the black vote, he posed with Pauline Pearce, who had famously ticked off the rioters in Hackney. In the *Telegraph*, the picture carried the headline: "Heroine backs Boris." However, she told the *Guardian*: "I didn't say I am backing Boris."

Boris failed to sparkle at that year's party conference, after Cameron introduced him with the line: "I don't know a four-letter word to describe him."

Ken Clarke had said ministers had been recording audio books for the blind. Speculating over the battle to succeed him, Cameron quipped that George Osborne "went straight for *The Man Who Would Be King*. I'm afraid Boris missed out. Instead he chose *The Joy of ... Sss ... Cycling*."

While Paxman gave him an easy ride, when he returned to the capital, Boris was greeted with a poster campaign by a dating agency that specialized in discrete encounters for the married. It featured a huge picture of Boris and carried the caption: "Affairs now guaranteed – no matter what you look like."

The Occupy London protesters were camped outside St Paul's Cathedral. One of their banners read: "Boris loves bankers." His response was to call on judges to have the "cojones" to kick the "crusties" out. He then claimed to be a crusty himself.

"It's an affectionate term from one crusty to another," he said, "and I wish them a Merry Crustmas." He also pointed out that their protest had not yet triggered the resignation of a single banker – while "three blameless clerics" had been "felled".

When Ken won approval with a promise to cut fares, Boris promised: "What I will not do is play politics with fares." Then when George Osborne stumped up £130 million, he did a quick U-turn.

He also came under criticism for his £4-million-a-mile cycling superhighways, which appeared to be nothing more than a line of blue paint that did nothing to protect their users. Indeed, two people died at one junction in 2011.

Though Boris's record in office was arguably thin, *GQ* hailed him "the most influential man in Britain". As Prime Minister, Cameron came in second. Another problem Boris had in the mayoral race was the speculation that he would run for parliament in the 2015 general election, which was a full year before his tenure of City Hall would run out. Boris told the BBC that there was "not a snowball's chance in Hades" that he would stand.

"I don't think I will do another big job in politics," he said.

The job of mayor was enough for him, though he found time to write *Johnson's Life of London*, which was soon recognized as a leadership manifesto. Meanwhile, he was ridiculing Cameron and Osborne's stance on the Euro crisis and even offering an alternative policy. Ken Livingstone joked that, in the mayoral election, he knew he could count on the vote of at least one Tory – the mayor himself.

Despite Boris's evident reluctance to spend another four years in City Hall, he won the election, albeit with a reduced majority. Two months later, the London Olympics gave him an international stage. He made a splash when he was left dangling from zip wire over Victoria Park waving Union Jacks.

Boris continued being what critics called a part-time mayor, writing his column for the *Telegraph*, though the £250,000 a year he got for it he told the BBC's *Hardtalk* was "chicken feed". In

February 2013, he was thrown out of a meeting of the London Assembly after calling the members "great supine protoplasmic invertebrate jellies". He pushed ahead with his plan to close down ticket offices on the Underground, providing an automated ticketing system instead, and promised a twenty-four-hour service at the weekends.

By March 2014, Boris's snowball seems to have survived its sojourn in Hell and he was looking for a London seat. In July, Sir John Randall, MP for the safe Conservative seat of Uxbridge and South Ruislip, said he would not be running in the general election. Boris was adopted as candidate there in September. The following month, he published his book *The Churchill Factor*. People drew their own conclusions.

By January 2015, with the election still four months away, the *Sunday Times* was reporting that Boris Johnson would be offered a cabinet post immediately if the Conservatives won – possibly a minister without portfolio until his term as mayor ran out.

Boris invited George Osborne over for lunch in his old constituency home near Thame. Afterwards they took a walk in the fields where they thrashed out a "peace pact" – Osborne would leave the way clear for Johnson to take on Theresa May for the leadership if Cameron was forced out.

The *Sunday Times* called this the "Thame cottage accord" and compared it to the Granita deal where Gordon Brown agreed to defer to Tony Blair over dinner at an Islington restaurant.

So, while Boris might not succeed in his ambition to become "world king", the leadership of the Conservative Party and, possibly, the premiership were within his grasp. Being President of the United States would have to wait a little longer.

Nevertheless, Boris prepared for his role as world statesman in typical fashion by callingISIS jihadis a bunch of porn-watching "wankers" who turn to violence because they "are not making it with girls…"

Meanwhile Boris awaits the call.

6729473R00074

Printed in Germany
by Amazon Distribution
GmbH, Leipzig